101
ARTS
&
CRAFTS
PROJECTS

Willard F. Wankelman
Bowling Green State University

Philip Wigg

wcb
Wm. C. Brown Publishers
Dubuque, Iowa

Cover photo by Bob Coyle

Copyright © 1961 by Willard F. Wankelman, Philip R. Wigg, and Marietta K. Wigg

Copyright © 1968, 1974, 1978, 1982, 1983, 1985 by Wm. C. Brown Publishers. All rights reserved

Library of Congress Catalog Card Number: 84–73464

ISBN 0 697 00748 0

Printed in the United States of America
10 9 8 7 6 5 4 3

contents

crayon   71

lettering   87

matting and framing   101

murals   109

paint and ink   115

paper and cardboard   135

preface

This revision of the trade edition of a classic handbook in the arts and crafts field contains a range of projects and techniques done in dozens of different media. Many of the projects are suitable for use with young children; others will challenge the older child or novice artist. The degree of complexity of most of the projects can be adjusted to the age and ability of the artist.

A special section in the front of the book gives practical tips and suggestions for making your own tools and materials. Use of homemade media and utensils is not only economical, but enhances the feeling that "I made it myself!"

Over a hundred craft projects are presented in the nine chapters—grouped according to medium. Each project includes a complete list of tools and materials, step-by-step instructions, illustrations of techniques and methods, and photographs of the project at various stages of completion. Samples of finished projects suggest ideas and themes.

This trade revision, newly titled 101 ARTS AND CRAFTS PROJECTS, presents a practical, easy-to-use guide for the adult to share with children (in groups or individually), or for the individual who is interested in finding new ideas for doing craft projects in a variety of mediums.

acknowledgments

We wish to express our appreciation to all who assisted in any way in the development of this edition. Their numbers are legion and they cannot all be identified.

Mrs. Jean Hasselschwert and her classes deserve a special debt of gratitude for the many fine illustrations they provided. Mrs. Hasselschwert also gave us enlightenment on the technicalities of some of the projects.

Tom Davenport was his usual witty and talented self.

Members of the Wm. C. Brown Company Publishers have been both demanding and helpful in expediting the production of this book.

formulas and hints

antique plaster finish

Soak the plaster in linseed oil. Remove and dust with dry umber or yellow ochre while still wet. Wipe off excess with a cloth until antique finish is obtained.

blown eggs

Raw, whole eggs can be emptied and the shells, when kept intact, can be decorated and used in many attractive ways.

With a needle, gently pierce a hole about the size of a grain of rice into both ends of a fresh raw egg at room temperature. Make sure the yolk is broken.

Blow hard into one end of egg, which is held over a bowl, and the contents will leave the other end. (Save for scrambled eggs.)

Let water run inside the egg shell and rinse well until all of the contents of the egg is removed. Allow it to dry before decorating.

The holes at each end can be covered with melted paraffin or candle wax applied with an old brush.

Proceed to decorate with dye, ribbon, decorative braid, crepe paper, colored tissue paper, paint, beads, etc.

Note: Wax crayon drawn or melted wax painted on the surface of the egg will resist colored dye for interesting effects.
Dye the light colors first, then add more wax and dye darker colors.
A larger opening may be made in the front of the egg by first coating the area to be cut away with colorless nail polish. The opening then may be cut with sharp nail scissors. If the egg cracks around the opening, this can be covered with beads, braid, etc.

A scene or decoration may then be glued in place inside the egg. Such decorative eggs are especially nice on the Christmas tree or Easter tree.

candle wax

Wax from an old candle is best.
Paraffin alone is good but melts rapidly.
Beeswax alone is excellent but expensive.
Mutton tallow makes excellent hard candles, but becomes rancid.
Two formulas that work well are:

1. 60% by weight of paraffin
     35% stearic acid
       5% beeswax
2. 10 oz. mutton tallow
     4 oz. beeswax
     2 oz. alum
     ½ oz. gum camphor

carving gesso

Mix whiting and shellac to consistency of thick cream and add powdered tempera as needed to color.

carving material

1 part modeling plaster
1 part sawdust

Mix ingredients. Pour into a cardboard box and allow to harden. Soak block in water if it becomes too hard to carve.

carving paste

5 parts whiting
1 part liquid glue

Mix with water, thinning to the consistency of cream, and add powdered tempera for color.

casting cement

3 parts sand
1 part portland cement

Mix with water to a smooth consistency.

encaustic paint

1 oz. beeswax
2 teaspoons dry pigment or dry tempera for each color

Heat the beeswax and stir in the color with a stick.
Transfer hot encaustic color to picture with brush, palette knife, etc. Wipe wax from brushes while still warm—turpentine or mineral spirits will act as a solvent.

felt applicator

A piece of felt held to a stick by a rubber band will ease application of chalk dust to a picture, and keep it a bit more permanent.

finger paint

1. 1 cup liquid starch
   6 cups water
   ½ cup soap chips (nondetergent)

   Dissolve the soap chips in the water until no lumps remain, then mix well with the starch and remaining water. Color with dry or wet tempera or food coloring.

2. Mix wheat paste (wallpaper paste) into cold or lukewarm water. Stir until smooth. Pour into containers, one for each color, and stir in color pigment.

3. Small pieces of colored chalk finely ground and added to paste of a smooth consistency makes an inexpensive finger paint.

4. Two qts. boiling water and 12 tbsp. starch first dissolved in cold water. Stir until thick. Pour into containers, one for each color, and add pigments and a few drops of oil of clove to prevent distressing odors. Keep in cool place.

5. Finger paint can be made from toothpaste or thick hand lotion and food coloring.

6. Mix non-detergent soap flakes, food coloring or dry tempera paint and water to a creamy consistency for an ideal finger paint.

7. Liquid starch mixed with tempera paint to a creamy consistency is also a suitable finger paint.

fixative (to keep work from smearing)

Dissolve gum arabic in water to the consistency of thin cream. Spray through an insect sprayer or atomizer. Commercial hair spray may also be used. Spray in well-ventilated areas.

glossy plaster finish

Dissolve white soap flakes in a pan or bowl to the consistency of thin cream.

Soak the plaster cast or carving thoroughly in the solution for at least thirty minutes. Remove and polish with a dry cloth.

Hyplar Modeling Paste

(M. Grumbacher, Inc., New York). This is a water-base paste, and dries and hardens quickly. It can be used for papier-mâché or can be modeled, shaped, carved, chiseled, or sawed when dry. The paste can be colored with acrylic watercolors that will dry to be waterproof.

Liquitex

(Permanent Pigments, Inc., Cincinnati, Ohio). A modeling paste with a water base, this is quick drying, and can be modeled, carved, tooled, textured, and tinted with acrylic watercolor paint that dries to be waterproof. Thinned with water, it can be used for papier-mâché.

Methylan Paste

(The Standard Chemical Products, Inc., Hoboken, N.J.). This water-base paste is colorless, odorless, nonstaining, nontoxic, and stays fresh indefinitely in a container that will not rust. It is suitable for use on papier-mâché, collage, découpage, etc. One-fourth pound makes approximately the same amount of paste as two pounds of wallpaper paste.

modeling cement

1 part portland cement
1 part asbestos cement
1 part powdered clay that has been sieved

Mix with water until of puttylike consistency.

nonsmearing chalk

Add six to eight tablespoons of sugar to an inch of water in a pan. Mix well until all of the sugar is dissolved. Soak chalk in the solution for ten to fifteen minutes. Draw with the chalk.

paint container

Paper milk containers stapled together with tops removed and with a cardboard handle make an ideal container for colored paint and water.

paint dispensing

Plastic mustard or ketchup containers make good paint dispensers. An aluminum nail in the top of each will keep the paint fresh. In some cases the plastic containers can be used for painting. Syrup pitchers make good paint dispensers and are ideal for storing paint.

parchment paper

Brush the surface of a piece of cream-colored manila paper with burnt linseed oil; brush the back of the paper with turpentine and allow to dry.

papier mâché

1 box Knox Gelatin
3 oz. white glue
2 oz. water
Mix ingredients and stir until mixture is smooth and creamy. Tissue paper or paper toweling strips, saturated with water, are placed over the object to the desired thickness. Will dry translucent and with a shiny surface.

plastic foam

6 tablespoons of plastic starch
1 cup dry detergent—for tinting, add powdered color

Mix with water and whip to consistency of marshmallow cream.

This can be used in decorating Christmas ornaments, puppet heads, etc.

Prang Media Mixer

(American Crayon Company, Sandusky, Ohio). This water-base mixer is a colorless, odorless, gelatinlike formula for converting liquid or dry tempera into colored finger paint. Used in a clear form, it will act as a binder for papier-mâché and as an adhesive for paper collage.

printing gimmicks

Glue heavy string or scraps of felt to a cardboard tube. Slip this tube over a painting roller so that it fits snugly. Roll it in paint and then over a piece of paper, possibly in various directions, to produce a design.

salt and cornstarch modeling mixture

1 cup salt
½ cup cornstarch
¾ cup water

Cook in an old double boiler and in two minutes this will form a glob or mass. Place the mass on wax paper until it is cool enough to handle, then knead (as bread dough) for three minutes. The material can be wrapped in foil until time for use. It will keep several days, but must be kneaded again before using. It works well around wire or armatures.

salt and flour modeling mixture

1 cup salt
1 cup flour
1 tablespoon powdered alum

Mix with water to consistency of putty.

salt and flour gesso

2 cups flour
1 cup salt
1 ½ to 2 cups water

Mix until it is smooth and does not stick to the fingers.

salt and flour relief mixture

3 parts salt
1 part flour

Mix with water for desired consistency.

salt and flour beads

2 parts table salt
1 part flour

Mix the salt and flour and water to a doughlike consistency. If color is desired, add dry pigment or food coloring. Break off small pieces and form into beads. Pierce each with a toothpick and allow to dry, then string.

sawdust and wheat paste for modeling

2 parts sawdust
1 part wheat paste

Add paste to cold water to form a smooth and creamy mixture. Add sawdust and more water if necessary, until paste becomes like putty.

silk screen paint

Combine liquid or powdered tempera mixed with a stiff mixture of soap flakes (not detergent) and warm water, or with Prang Media Mixer (mentioned earlier in this section).

simulated marble

1 part Vermiculite
1 part modeling plaster

Mix ingredients and add water, stirring constantly until the mixture becomes creamy. Pour in cardboard box and allow to harden. Model with knife, rasp, sandpaper, or any similar tool.

simulated stone

Formula A
1 part sand
1 part cement
4 parts Zonalite
1 part modeling plaster

Mix ingredients, then add water to form a thick paste. Pour into cardboard, and allow to harden.

Formula B
2 parts sand
2 parts cement
4 parts Zonalite

Mix ingredients, then add water to form a thick paste. Pour into cardboard and allow to harden.

soda and cornstarch modeling mixture

1 cup cornstarch
2 cups baking soda
1 ¼ cups water
Food coloring
Aluminum foil or plastic bag

Combine the first three ingredients in a saucepan and cook over medium heat, stirring constantly. When the mixture is thickened to doughlike consistency, turn out on a piece of aluminum foil or on a breadboard. Food coloring may be worked into the clay when it has cooled slightly.

Keep the clay in a refrigerator covered with aluminum foil or in a plastic bag to keep it pliable when not in use.

Clay may be rolled and cut into shapes or may be modeled into small shapes.

synthetic oil paint

Add dry color to regular wheat paste that has been mixed to thin, smooth consistency. Apply with a stiff brush.

tempera paint for glossy surfaces

Liquid detergent, or a few drops of glycerine mixed with tempera paint, enables the paint to adhere to shiny or oily surfaces, such as aluminum foil, glass, etc.

translucent paper

2 parts turpentine
1 part linseed oil

Brush or wipe the mixture on the paper and allow it to dry.

transparent paper

Two parts linseed oil and one part turpentine applied to the back of a drawing with a brush or rag will cause the illustration to become transparent.

Zonalite sculpture cement

1 part cement
5 parts Zonalite

Mix cement and Zonalite with water until smooth. Pour into a cardboard box or mold to harden. Zonalite cement is lightweight and can be cut with a saw or carved with any metal tool.

ceramics

clay modeling

procedure

Method A
1. Beginning with a basic shape of the object to be modeled, squeeze or push the clay to form the features (legs, arms, head, etc.). Think of the object as a whole, rather than as separate parts.
2. Between working sessions, wrap with a moist cloth to retain plasticity.
3. Allow the piece to dry slowly at room temperature.
4. Check pages 7 and 8 for firing details.

Method B
1. Beginning with a basic shape of the object to be modeled, use a modeling tool to carve away all unnecessary parts until the piece is formed.

Note: Combining parts or sections is another method of modeling, but not recommended for children. Assembling parts is very important, and unless the two pieces of clay are of the same consistency and combined together properly, they will shrink irregularly in drying.

1　　　　　　　　　　　　　　2　　　　　　　　　　　　　　3

clay tiles

procedure

1. Knead (wedge) the clay to a workable consistency.
2. Spread the damp cloth on a smooth table top.
3. Place the two sticks on the damp cloth parallel to each other. The space between the sticks will be the width of the finished tile.
4. Roll a ball of clay and place it between the sticks (Ill. 1).
5. Flatten the clay by running the rolling pin along the parallel sticks. The clay will be flattened to the thickness of the sticks (Ill. 2).
6. Cut the slab of clay into tiles, and allow it to become almost dry, or leather-hard (Ill. 3).
7. Plan a design on thin paper, the size of the clay tile.
8. When the clay is almost dry, place the paper design over the tile and transfer the design by retracing the lines with a sharp pencil or instrument.
9. The following three methods of decoration are possible:

    A. Incised—scratch the design into the leather-hard clay with a sharp tool.
    B. Relief—carve away the background areas and allow the design to stand out.
    C. Inlaid—carve out areas of the design and replace with clay of a different color, making sure both clays are of the same consistency.

10. See pages 7 and 8 for firing details.

supplies

1. Local or commercial water-base clay
2. Rolling pin
3. Two sticks, one-half inch thick
4. Damp cloth
5. Knife or scissors
6. Thin paper
7. Sharp pencil

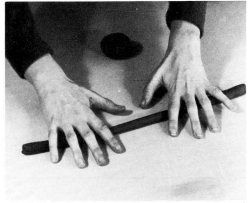

1   2   3

coil pot

supplies

1. Local or commercial water base clay
2. Modeling tool
3. Small container for mixing slip

procedure

Method A

Coils built on a pinch pot base as done by the American Indians

1. Knead (wedge) the clay to a workable consistency.
2. Roll a ball of pliable clay between the palms of the hands to form a sphere approximately the size of a small orange.
3. Hold the sphere in the fingers of both hands. The thumb should be free to press the clay to form the pot. Keep thumbs pointed up and form the pot upside down.
4. Press the thumbs gently into the center of the sphere and at the same time press with the fingers on the outside while rotating the ball of clay (Ill. 1).
5. Continue pressing with both the fingers and the thumbs while rotating the clay until the ball is hollowed and the walls are of uniform thickness (approximately one-half of an inch). Cracks may appear if the clay is too dry, or if pressed into shape too quickly or forcefully. Repair any such cracks immediately by gently rubbing the fingers over the clay until they disappear.
6. The pot, if built correctly, will not have any flat areas. To flatten the bottom of the pot, hold it gently between the fingers with both hands and tap it lightly on a table top.
7. Roll another piece of clay into round strips or coils of approximately one-half of an inch in diameter, making sure the strip makes a complete turn to insure its roundness (Ill. 2).
8. Scratch the top edge of the pinch pot base (Ill. 3) and apply a thin coat of slip (liquid clay) over the scratches (Ill. 4). The slip helps the coil adhere to the pinch pot base.
9. Place the coil on the slip-covered edge of the base (Ill. 5). Cut both ends at the same angle so that they fit snugly (Ill. 6). Gently press the coil to the base and fuse the joint both on the outside and inside (Ill. 7).
10. Scratch the top edge of the first coil, apply slip (Ill. 8) and add the second coil. Remember to fit the ends together tightly. Gently press the second coil to the first coil and fuse them together.
11. Repeat procedure ten until the coils create a completed form.
12. Allow the pot to dry slowly at room temperature.
13. See pages 7 and 8 for firing suggestions.

4

5

6

7

8

9

Method B

1. Knead (wedge) the clay to a workable consistency.
2. Roll the clay into round strips or coils of approximately one-half of an inch in diameter, making sure the strip makes a complete turn to insure its roundness (Ill. 2).
3. Wind the strip into a tight coil to the desired size for the base. Fuse the coil together with a small tool or the fingers until all traces of the round strip disappear (Ill. 9). A ball of clay flattened on a damp cloth to approximately one-half of an inch thickness also makes a cloth to approximately one-half of an inch thickness also makes a good base for a pot when cut to the desired diameter.
4. Scratch the outside top edge of the base and apply a thin coat of slip (liquid clay) over the scratches. The slip helps the base adhere to the first coil.
5. Place another coil on the slip-covered edge of the base. Cut both ends at the same angle so they fit snugly. Gently press the coil to the base and fuse the joint both on the outside and inside.
6. Scratch the top edge of the first coil, apply slip and add the second coil. Remember to fit the ends together tightly. Gently press the second coil to the first coil and fuse them together.
7. Repeat procedure six until the coils create a complete form.
8. Allow the pot to dry slowly at room temperature.
9. See pages 7 and 8 for firing details.

folded clay animals

supplies

1. Local or commercial water-base clay
2. Rolling pin
3. Cloth
4. Knife
5. Two flat sticks, one-half inch thick
6. Paper, pencil, and scissors

procedure

1. Knead (wedge) the clay to a workable consistency.
2. Spread a damp cloth on a smooth table top. Place the two sticks parallel to each other on the damp cloth. The distance between the sticks will determine the size of the finished animal.
3. Roll a ball of clay between the palms of the hands to form a sphere and place it between the sticks.
4. Flatten the ball of clay by running the rolling pin along the parallel sticks. The thickness of the clay is determined by the thickness of the sticks.
5. Draw an animal on a piece of paper that is the size of the clay slab. If desired, the drawing can be scratched directly on the clay.
6. Cut the animal pattern out of the paper and place it on the slab of clay.
7. Hold the paper in place and cut the clay with a knife, following the outline of the pattern (Ill. 1).
8. Gently remove the clay animal from the slab and curve it into position (Ill. 2). The legs will be bent down to make it a self-supporting unit. Parts of the clay animal can be twisted into various attitudes.
9. Smooth out any rough edges and add textures or features with any modeling tool.
10. If the clay is too soft to support itself, prop it up with a wad of paper or clay.
11. Allow the animal to dry slowly at room temperature (Ill. 3).
12. See pages 7 and 8 for firing suggestions.

1

2

3

kilns

Clay pieces that have just been completed are called *greenware* and should dry naturally before being fired in a kiln. Artificial heat is likely to cause the piece to crack. All decorations must be completed on the product before the piece is completely dry.

When the clay is completely dry (bone dry), it is ready to be placed in the kiln for firing. Firing will not only vitrify, or fuse, the clay but will burn out any impurities.

There are numerous kilns of all sizes, shapes, and prices, which are fueled with gas, oil, coal, or electricity. Small electric table model kilns that will operate on 110 to 115 volts and have a front door opening are suggested; and they, too, come in various sizes (Ill. 1.)

The inside firing chambers of table model kilns have a large range and usually a maximum of 2300°F, which is more than adequate. Several inside firing chamber sizes of electric table model kilns are:

6 ¼″ wide, 7″ deep, 4″ high
6″ wide, 6″ deep, 6″ high
8″ wide, 10″ deep, 4″ high
10″ wide, 12″ deep, 5″ high
10″ wide, 9″ deep, 10″ high
10″ wide, 10″ deep, 9″ high

Larger electric kilns will in all probability use 220 volt current.

1

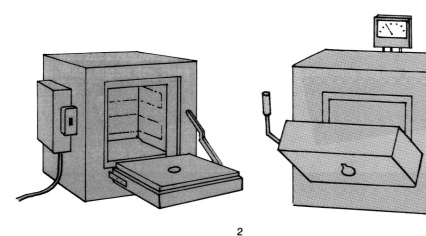

2   3

supplies

1. Kiln
2. Kiln shelves
3. Shelf supports
4. Kiln furniture (stilts, triangles)
5. Pyrometric cones
6. Kiln wash (Glaze drippings are easily removed from shelves coated with kiln wash.)
7. Kiln cement (for repairing cracks and chips in kiln wall)

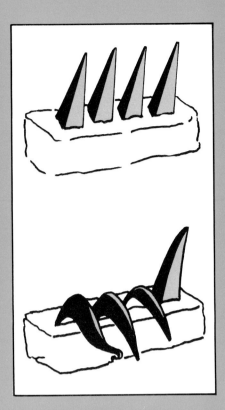

Cone Temperature Chart

Pyrometric Cones

	Fahrenheit	Centigrade		Fahrenheit	Centigrade
Cone 018	1328	720	Cone 05	1904	1040
Cone 016	1463	795	Cone 04	1940	1060
Cone 015	1481	805	Cone 03	2039	1115
Cone 014	1526	830	Cone 02	2057	1125
Cone 013	1580	860	Cone 01	2093	1145
Cone 012	1607	875	Cone 1	2120	1160
Cone 011	1643	894	Cone 2	2129	1165
Cone 010	1661	905	Cone 3	2138	1170
Cone 09	1706	930	Cone 4	2174	1190
Cone 08	1742	949	Cone 5	2201	1205
Cone 07	1814	990	Cone 6	2246	1230
Cone 06	1859	1015			

Temperature equivalents figured at firing rate of 300°F or 149°C per hour.

Some kilns will have a switch control for low, medium, and high temperatures (Ill. 2) Some will come equipped with a pyrometer, an indicator for reading the kiln temperature (Ill. 3). These extras are ideal, but much cheaper and equally accurate are pyrometric cones (Ill. 4), which are used to indicate fusion.

Three or four of these cones with different fusing points are placed at a slight angle to one of their faces (not on their edge) in a piece of pliable clay (Ill. 4). The clay is allowed to dry, then placed in the kiln so the cones can be seen through the spy hole in the kiln door. A piece of fire brick may be necessary to lift the cones high enough to be seen.

The kiln will heat slowly and a periodic check of the cones through the spy hole will let you know the approximate temperature of the heat as the cones begin to melt. When the last cone (Ill. 5) is beginning to melt, the kiln can be turned off, as the desired temperature has been attained.

A piece fired only once is called *bisque,* or biscuit ware, and it can be glazed and fired again. A glaze will give the pieces a glasslike finish. Glazes can be purchased from a commercial company that will give instructions for use and the temperature cone at which the glaze matures. (Avoid any glazes not certified by the manufacturer as being free of lead and nontoxic.) The glaze is applied by spraying, brushing, or dipping. Dipping a piece in and out of a bowl of glaze may be the most practical method. Fingermarks are removed by daubing glaze on the spots with a brush.

making clay

Any local clay can be easily transformed into pliable clay by the following method. This same method is used in reconditioning any unfired clay.

procedure

1. Break the moist clay into small pieces and allow them to dry thoroughly.
2. Place the pieces of dry clay into the cloth bag and pound them with the hammer or mallet until they are almost powder.
3. Fill the container half full of water and pour the broken or powdered clay into it until the clay rises above the surface of the water. Moist clay will not disintegrate when placed in water, so be sure it is bone dry and broken into pieces. The smaller the pieces, the more quickly the dissolving process will take place. This process is called *slaking*.
4. Allow the clay to soak for at least an hour. This period will vary according to the size of the pieces.
5. Stir the clay thoroughly with a stick or the hands until all the lumps are dissolved. This clay mixture is called *slip*.
6. Pour the slip into the second container through the sieve to remove any foreign matter and allow it to stand overnight. If there is any excess clear water, pour it off.
7. Remove any excess moisture by placing the clay on the plaster slab. Allow the water to be absorbed until the clay can be kneaded without sticking to the hands.
8. Store the clay in a container with a lid, or cover the container with a damp cloth. Small amounts of clay can be kept moist by using plastic bags or aluminum foil.

suggestions on handling water clay

1. Pliable clay should be kneaded (wedged) to remove all air bubbles before working.
2. Clay objects should dry slowly to prevent cracking. Thinner forms will dry more quickly than thicker forms. The thin form may be wrapped with a damp cloth to equalize the drying.
3. Cover the clay objects with a damp cloth or plastic bag to slow the drying process, or to keep the clay moist from day to day.
4. Moist clay will not adhere to dry clay due to shrinkage.
5. Clay appendages, or details that are to be added to pots or figures, must be of the same consistency as the piece to which they are to be attached. The two areas that are to be joined should be scratched with a tool, and covered with a slip (liquid clay) before being placed together. Then, the joints should be fused into one piece with a smooth tool or the fingers.
6. If hanging plaques are to be made, carve or pierce any holes while the clay is leather-hard.
7. Dry clay objects (unfired clay is called greenware) must be fired to a temperature of at least 1500°F, or 830°C, to be hardened. An electric kiln is the best method for firing. However, the primitive method of an open campfire can be utilized.

supplies

1. Local or commercial water-base clay
2. Two containers for mixing clay (galvanized or plastic buckets, crocks, earthenware crocks, etc. A tightly fitting lid is desirable.)
3. Hammer or mallet
4. Cloth bag
5. Sieve, or piece of window screen
6. Plastic bags or aluminum foil for storing clay
7. A plaster slab is ideal for absorbing excess moisture from the clay

8. Glaze can be applied to bisque (a piece of clay that has been fired once is called bisque) by dipping, spraying, or with a brush. The piece is then refired. All glaze must be wiped from the bottom or the foot of the piece with a sponge or cloth before firing.

9. A simple, low-fire glaze can be purchased commercially.

10. If no kiln is available, the greenware can be finished by waxing, painting with enamel, shellac, or varnish, or with tempera paint. Clear plastic spray, varnish, or shellac can be applied over the tempera paint for permanency.

11. Slip (liquid clay) of different colors can be painted on damp-ware for decoration. The piece must then be dried and fired.

12. Overhandling of the clay will cause it to dry rapidly, which in turn causes cracks or crumbling.

pinch pot

procedure

1. Knead (wedge) the clay until it is of a workable consistency and the air bubbles have been removed.
2. Roll a ball of pliable clay between the palms of the hands to form a sphere approximately the size of a small orange.
3. Hold the sphere in the fingers of both hands. The thumb should be free to press the clay to form the pot. Keep the thumbs pointed up and form the pot upside down. (See Ill. 1, p. 32).
4. Press the thumbs gently into the center of the sphere and at the same time press with the fingers on the outside while rotating the ball of clay.
5. Continue pressing with both the fingers and thumbs while rotating the clay until the ball is hollowed and the walls are of uniform thickness (approximately one-half of an inch). Cracks may appear if the clay is too dry or if it is pressed into shape too quickly or forcefully. Repair any such cracks immediately by gently rubbing the fingers over the clay until they disappear.
6. The finished pot, if built correctly, will not have any flat areas. To flatten the bottom of the pot, hold it gently between the fingers with both hands and tap it lightly on a table top.
7. Press the end of a key, hairpin, paper clip, etc., into the top edge of the pot, creating a single and interesting decoration.
8. Allow the pinch pot to dry slowly at room temperature.
9. See pages 7 and 8 for firing details.

1. Local or commercial water base clay

1

2

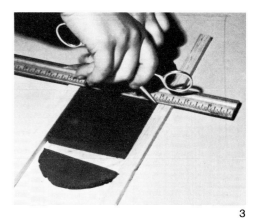
3

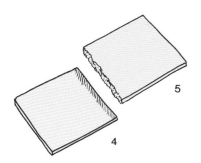
4

5

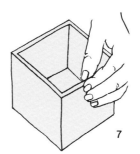
6

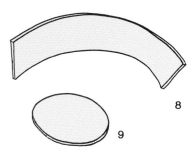
7

8

9

slab pot

A slab pot is built with flat pieces of clay which are joined together to form a container.

supplies

1. Local or commercial water-base clay
2. Rolling pin
3. Two sticks, approximately one-half inch thick and twelve to twenty inches long
4. Damp cloth
5. Knife or scissors
6. Water container for mixing slip
7. Cardboard pattern

procedure

1. Knead (wedge) the clay to a workable consistency.
2. Spread the damp cloth on a smooth table top.
3. Place the two sticks on the damp cloth, parallel to each other. The space between the sticks will be the width of the finished tile.
4. Roll a ball of clay and place it between the sticks (Ill. 1).
5. Flatten the clay by running the rolling pin along the parallel sticks (Ill. 2). The clay will be flattened to the thickness of the sticks.
6. Place cardboard pattern over flattened clay. Using it as a guide, cut around pattern with a knife (Ill. 3).
7. Using the same cardboard pattern, cut three more slabs and allow to stiffen to a leather-hard condition.
8. To assemble a pot, score the edge of each slab with a knife (Ill. 4).
9. Put slip on scored edge (Ill. 5) and place two pieces together.
10. Prepare a small roll of clay and press into the joint of each corner (Ill. 6). Continue this procedure until all four sides are together and smoothed inside and out.
11. Score the edges of a fifth piece, which will be the bottom.
12. Press the four sides on the bottom and complete (Ill. 7).

A cylindrical slab pot is made from one slab (Ill. 8) placed on a round base (Ill. 9).
Decorations can be done with a syringe filled with slip of a different color. Squeeze syringe and trail design.
Stamp any design in leather-hard clay.

chalk

nature of the medium

chalk and pastel

The original chalks for drawing, some still in use today, were pure earth, cut and shaped into implements. The addition of a binder created a fabricated chalk that we know as pastel. Sanguine Conté closely approximates the pure earth material. Chalks used by the early masters were generally limited to reds (sanguine), black, and white. These colors have been greatly increased in number.

Some artists apply chalks in separate strokes, letting the color blending take place in the viewer's eye. Others are not reluctant to blend the colors, and do so successfully, although there is a danger of the colors being muddied. Of course, there is no need to caution children against this; they should be encouraged to explore by rubbing with fingers, stumps, cotton swabs, anything available. Most children will select and use chalks fearlessly.

Chalk drawing is best done on a paper with "tooth," or a slightly coarse, abrasive surface. This texture helps the paper trap and hold the chalk particles. Many papers have this character, including the inexpensive manila.

Chalks are brittle and easily broken. They are also impermanent, smearing very easily. Completed works should be sprayed with a protective fixative; this should be done with optimum ventilation.

Chalks possessing strong color and binding ingredients should not be used on chalkboards—they are nearly indelible.

Chalk strokes can be strengthened, and their character altered, by wetting the chalk or paper. Various liquids have been used experimentally with interesting results, including dipping the chalk sticks in buttermilk, starch, and sugar water.

chalk and carbon paper

procedure

1. Draw picture design on paper with colored chalk.
2. Place carbon paper face down on chalk drawing.
3. Run hand over carbon paper to transfer chalk drawing to carbon paper.
4. Remove carbon paper and spray with clear spray to keep from smearing.

supplies

1. Paper
2. Carbon paper
3. Chalk
4. Clear spray

The above illustrations are chalk drawings.

The above illustrations are carbon paper prints.

chalk and string design

supplies

1. String
2. Chalk
3. Soft wooden board
4. Thumbtacks
5. Paper
6. Plastic spray or fixative

procedure

1. Press a tack into the board.
2. Tie string to the tack.
3. Rub the string with a piece of chalk.
4. Place the string over a sheet of paper, pull the string taut with one hand, and snap the string against the paper with the other hand.
5. Move the paper into different positions and repeat steps three and four after each movement of the paper.

Note: Assorted colors may be rubbed against the strings. Lines may be intentionally blurred by stroking. Shapes bounded by the lines may be colored in to create a more definite pattern. The chalk should be "fixed" to the paper with a protective coating of clear plastic spray or fixative.

chalk and tempera paint

procedure

1. Make a light pencil outline drawing on paper.
2. Mix tempera or latex paint to the consistency of cream.
3. Dip end of desired colored chalk into chosen color of paint.
4. Apply paint with chalk stick in brushlike strokes.
5. Continue until picture is completed.
6. Detail can be added with plain chalk.
7. Protect the picture with transparent spray.

supplies

1. Chalk
2. Tempera, or latex paint
3. Paper
4. Clear spray

chalk and tempera print

procedure

1. Complete a design or drawing with colored chalk on a piece of good quality paper. Be sure to use the chalk heavily.
2. Coat another piece of paper of the same size with white tempera paint. Use a large brush and paint in both directions to smooth the paint over one entire side.
3. While the tempera is still wet, place the chalk drawing face down in the tempera paint.
4. Rub firmly over the paper with fingers and/or the hand.
5. Separate the two papers before they are dry.
6. Two prints will result—the chalk will have merged with the paint on both prints (Ills. 1, 2).
7. Experiments with different colors will produce numerous effects.

supplies

1. Chalk
2. Tempera paint
3. Paper
4. Large brush

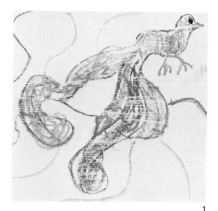

1

2

chalk painting

procedure

1. Mix six or eight tablespoons of sugar into a small amount of water until disolved into a thin solution.
2. Soak the chalk sticks in the sugar water solution for ten to fifteen minutes.
3. Use soaked chalk stick as a paint brush.
4. When chalk strokes become hard and dry the chalk will not rub.

chalk on sandpaper

procedure

1. Draw with the chalk on the sandpaper. The rough surface of the sandpaper will help to achieve rich and vivid textural effects.

Note: Greater richness of color can be achieved if the sandpaper is moist. It will also attract and hold greater quantities of rich chalk color.

chalk, tempera, and starch print

supplies

1. Liquid starch
2. Powder tempera
3. Brush
4. A scratching instrument—
   a stick, a spoon, etc.
5. Colored chalk
6. Two sheets of paper

procedure

1. Mix the liquid starch and tempera paint to produce a dripless paint (Ill. 1).
2. Brush the mixture on a sheet of paper (Ill. 2).
3. Scratch a design in the wet paint (Ill. 3).
4. Coat another sheet of paper with colored chalk (Ill. 4).
5. Place the second sheet, chalk side down, over the wet paint surface (Ill. 5).
6. Lightly rub the back of the top sheet (Ill. 6).
7. Pull off the top sheet.

chalk textures

procedure

1. Hold a thin paper against a surface that has a definite texture and rub the chalk over the paper. The texture will be transferred to the paper by the chalk.
2. Place the paper against another texture and transfer it to another portion of the paper.
3. Textures may be overlapped.

Note: A number of suggested textural surfaces are shown below. Chalk is easily smeared; and the completed drawing should have some protection. Commercially manufactured transparent sprays and fixatives are of some help, as is a home recipe to be found on page viii. Use sprays with optimum ventilation.

supplies

1. Chalk
2. Thin drawing paper
3. Pencil or crayon
4. Textured surfaces

drawing with chalk

1. Chalks
2. Colored paper
3. Fixative, or clear plastic spray
4. Insect sprayer or atomizer for application of fixative over chalk

procedure

1. *Light chalks on dark papers*
   This type of drawing is helpful in aiding the child to interpret subjects that are light in value, such as snowscapes, snowmen, polar bears, spring flowers. The chalk and dark paper produces good contrast in tone and brilliance of color.

2. *Chalk on grey paper*
   A middle-tone grey paper allows for good contrasts in both light and dark chalks. This contrast is developed most effectively if some of the paper is allowed to show through.

3. *Chalk on colored paper*
   Subtle and bold contrasts may be achieved, depending on the colors chosen.

shading with chalk dust

procedure

1. Scrape the tool along the side of the chalk sticks to produce dust. The dust particles from the chalk may be scraped directly onto areas of drawings done in other media. The cotton can be used to blend the dust in tonal passages which will enrich the original drawing.

Note: Chalk is easily smeared, and the completed drawing should have some protection. Commercially manufactured transparent sprays and fixatives are of some help, as is a home recipe to be found on page viii. Use sprays with optimum ventilation.

1. Chalk
2. Flat, hard tool for scraping
3. Cotton, face tissue, or chalk applicator

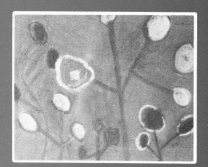

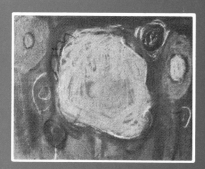

supplies

1. Colored chalks
2. Wet paper

wet paper chalk drawing

procedure

1. Draw over the damp paper with the chalk. The colors will generally be brighter and more exciting than those applied to dry paper. It is possible to use wet and dry techniques on one drawing by painting plain water over some areas prior to drawing. If the paper is not of fairly heavy stock, there is a danger of irregular wrinkling and curling.

Note: Soaking chalk sticks for ten minutes in a strong solution of sugar water before use reduces the tendency to smear. Commercially manufactured transparent sprays and fixatives are of some help, as is a home recipe to be found on page viii. Use sprays with optimum ventilation.

crafts

beads from
soda and cornstarch mixture

supplies

1. 1 cup cornstarch
2. 2 cups baking soda (1 lb. box)
3. 1¼ cups water
4. Saucepan
5. Stove or hot plate
6. Aluminum foil
7. Food coloring
8. Plastic bag
9. Watercolors or tempera paint
10. Clear commercial spray
11. Ball of clay (not necessary, but good for drying beads)— a piece of styrofoam could serve the same purpose
12. Toothpicks
13. Rolling pin or glass jar

procedure

1. Combine the ingredients one cup cornstarch, two cups baking soda, one and one-fourth cup water in a saucepan. Cook over medium heat, stirring constantly.
2. When the mixture is thickened to doughlike consistency, turn out on a piece of aluminum foil or breadboard.
3. Food coloring may be worked into the clay when it has cooled slightly.
4. Keep the clay in a refrigerator, covered with aluminum foil or plastic to keep it pliable when not in use.
5. Pinch off a lump of the mixture and shape into a bead. Spheres and cylinders can be formed easily by rolling the mixture between the palms of the hands.
6. Roll out the mixture flat with a rolling pin or glass jar and cut flat beads from it.
7. Punch a hole through each bead with a toothpick. Leave the toothpicks in the beads and stick them into the ball of clay for drying. Turn the toothpicks in the beads occasionally to keep them from sticking.
8. Shellac the beads and, when they are dry, string them.

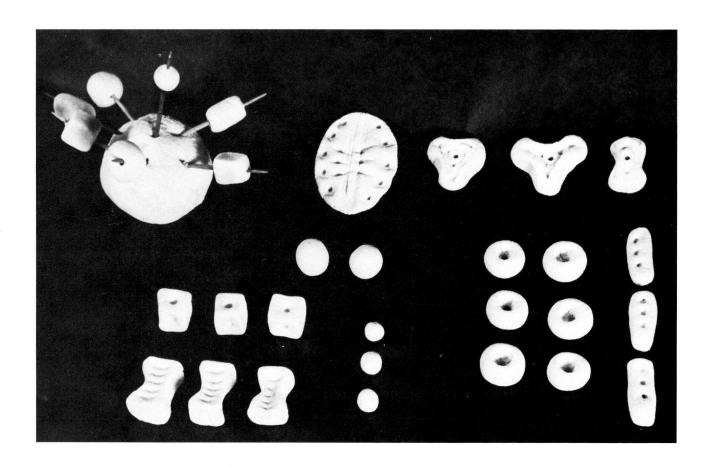

bleach painting

procedure

1. Place colored paper on several thicknesses of newspaper.
2. Draw picture with cotton swab dipped in liquid bleach. Give careful supervision to the use of the bleach.
3. The bleach will lighten the paper in seconds.
4. Allow the colored papers to dry separately from the newspaper.
5. Other media, such as markers, oil pastels, crayons, and/or ink may be added to the picture when the bleach is dry.

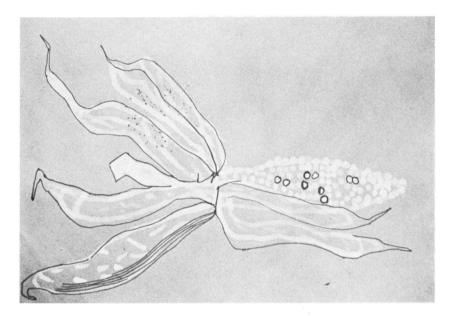

cardboard bracelets

supplies

1. Cardboard tube
2. Contact paper or tissue paper
3. Starch or paste
4. Tempera, or latex paint
5. Brush
6. Clear spray

procedure

1. Cut cardboard tube into rings.
2. If tube will not fit over hand, cut out a section so that it will slip over the hand.
3. Wrap each ring with contact paper.
4. If contact paper is not available, cover the ring with tissue paper that has been soaked in a solution of starch or diluted paste.
5. Decorate with paint.
6. Spray with clear spray. Use sprays with optimum ventilation.

Note: String and other materials may be glued to the bracelet before finishing.

collage

Collage is a French word similar to collé except that materials of all kinds are admissible to the picture. Painted and drawn passages may be combined with scrap materials to create a desired effect.

procedure

1. Arrange these items into a design or picture.
2. When satisfied, paste or glue on the cardboard background.
3. Any necessary details can be added with crayons or paints.

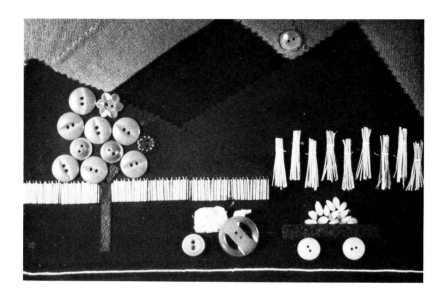

supplies

1. Piece of cardboard
2. A collection of items most of which might be discarded (small scraps of cloth and textured paper, bottle caps, buttons, toothpicks, sand, pebbles, soda straws, string, yarn, rope, used sandpaper, etc.). Use only those items that can be adhered with some permanency to the cardboard.
3. Scissors
4. Paste or glue

edible cookies

supplies

1. Wax paper
2. Rolling pin
3. Sharply pointed knife
4. Small brush
5. Cookie sheet
6. Wire rack
7. Pancake turner
8. Three large bowls
9. Four or five small fruit glasses for cookie paint
10. Recipe

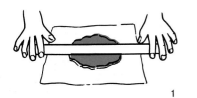

procedure

1. Cookie recipe:
   4 cups sifted flour
   2 teaspoons baking powder
   ¾ cups butter or margarine (1½ sticks)
   1½ cups sugar
   1 teaspoon salt
   2 eggs
   2 teaspoons vanilla
   1 teaspoon lemon extract

   Cookie paint:
   5 egg yolks
   2 teaspoons water
   food coloring

2. Sift flour, baking powder, and salt into one bowl.
3. In second bowl, beat butter with sugar until light and fluffy.
4. Beat in eggs, vanilla, and lemon extract.
5. Stir in approximately one-third of flour mixture at a time.
6. Repeat until a stiff dough results.
7. Moisten table top and cover with wax paper (moisture will keep paper from slipping).
8. Roll out a portion of dough on the wax paper to a thickness of one-fourth inch (Ill. 1).
9. Cut out desired shapes with sharp knife and trim away excess dough (Ill. 2). Cardboard patterns previously cut can be used.
10. Transfer cut cookies with pancake turner to lightly greased cookie sheet.
11. Repeat process with remaining dough.
12. To make cookie paint colors, beat egg yolks with water in bowl.
13. Divide egg yolk mixture into fruit glasses, one glass for each color to be used.
14. Add several drops of various food colors into each glass until desired color is obtained.
15. With a small brush, decorate each cookie. Make sure the paint is spread thickly to prevent cracking during baking (Ill. 3).
16. Place cookie sheet into moderate oven (375°) and bake cookies for ten minutes, or until dough is firm and light golden in color in unpainted areas.
17. Move cookies to wire rack until cool.

Note: By placing colored lifesavers in openings cut in the cookies, transparent windows will be produced when baked. If the cookies are to be hung the openings should be cut out before baking (Ill. 4).

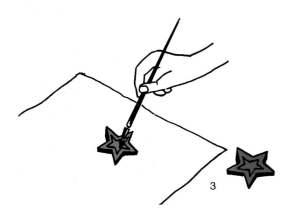

embossed metal

procedure

1. Cut the foil to the size of the finished work.
2. Develop a design on paper, the same size as the piece of foil.
3. Place the drawing on the foil and transfer the design by retracing the line with a pencil, pressing hard enough to make an impression.
4. Place the foil on a pad of newspaper or cloth. Decide which areas of the design are to be raised, and with a suitable tool (large, small, pointed, etc.) begin to press the foil into shape. Emboss the foil from both sides to avoid crinkling the metal. Remove the pad, place on a smooth hard surface, and work around the raised portions to flatten the background.
5. Copper foil can be oxidized by painting the design with ammonium sulphide until the entire surface is darkened. Wash the foil under running water and dry it. The ammonium sulphide will create an unpleasant odor.
6. Clean and polish the foil with steel wool. The oxidizing will remain in the low areas.
7. Lacquer or clear plastic spray applied to the copper or brass foil will keep it from tarnishing. Use sprays with optimum ventilation.

Note: Numerous textures can be embossed to give richness to the modeling. Enamel or lacquer will adhere to the foil to add color.

supplies

1. Copper, aluminum, or brass foil
2. Modeling tool (anything that will not cut through or scratch the metal, such as spoon, pencil, sharpened wooden dowel, etc.)
3. Fine steel wool
4. Pencil and paper
5. Pad of newspaper or cloth (a turkish towel is excellent)
6. Oxidizing liquid (ammonium sulphide—a very unpleasant odor is produced, and adequate ventilation is recommended)
7. Clear plastic spray or lacquer (not necessary for aluminum)

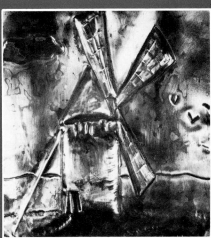

embossed modeling paste

supplies

1. Heavy cardboard
2. Strong paper
3. Pencil
4. Modeling paste
5. Modeling tool (any blunt instrument, nail, knitting needle, orange stick, etc.)
6. Ink, watercolor, or tempera paint
7. Brush
8. Shellac, varnish, or clear plastic spray
9. Glue or rubber cement

procedure

1. Cut a piece of heavy drawing paper slightly larger than the size of the finished work (Ill. 1).
2. Create a pencil drawing on the paper (Ill. 2).
3. Place finished drawing face down.
4. Cut a piece of heavy cardboard at least one-half-inch smaller than the paper on all sides and place over drawing (Ill. 3).
5. Cut off the four corners of the paper (Ill. 4), to enable the paper to fold back against the cardboard.
6. Lift the cardboard and cover one side with a smooth layer of modeling paste to a thickness of approximately one-sixteenth-inch. (Spread the paste with a stick or strip of cardboard.)
7. Place the modeling pasted surface of the cardboard face down on the drawing paper (Ill. 4).
8. Turn one-half-inch border of the drawing paper to the back of the cardboard and secure with glue or rubber cement.
9. Allow to dry long enough so that the drawing can be modeled with any blunt tool. (The paper will puncture if it is not dry enough.)
10. Paint the drawing when dry (Ill. 5).
11. A protective coating of shellac, varnish, or clear plastic spray can be added to the finished plaque. Use sprays with optimum ventilation.

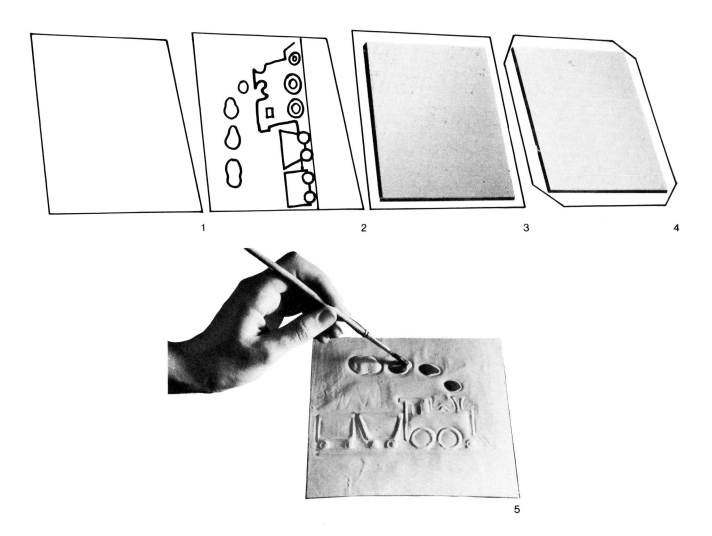

1   2   3   4

5

fabric crayons

procedure

1. Draw a design on white paper with a pencil.
2. Color the design with fabric crayons, using considerable pressure.
3. Remove any loose crayon specks and turn the paper design face down on the synthetic cloth which is on an ironing pad of several layers of paper.
4. Apply the iron to the design, holding it in place for thirty seconds. Lift the iron and move it to the untransferred areas of the design. If the iron is moved excessively the design may blur. The iron should be on the "cotton" setting and allowed to heat up.
5. "Sneak a peek" by holding the design and lifting one corner to check the strength of the color and design. Apply the heat until the design is completely transferred.

Note: Pillows, wall hangings, table cloths, soft sculptures, banners, and clothing are all possibilities with fabric crayons. Articles can be machine washed using warm water and gentle action. Do not use a bleach or put the work in a dryer. The color can be reapplied and the design used again.

supplies

1. Fabric crayons
2. White paper
3. Synthetic cloth
4. Newspaper
5. Iron (with no steam vents)

gesso plate

supplies

1. Commercial dry-ground gesso (or see formula on page 247)
2. Hot plate and old double boiler
3. Paper plates
4. Shellac, varnish, or clear plastic spray
5. Brush
6. Tempera paint or enamel paint

procedure

1. Mix the gesso according to the directions on the can, or see formula on page 247.
2. Paint two or three paper plates on both sides with the gesso, which should be the consistency of heavy cream.
3. Press the plates together while still wet, making sure the edges fit tightly. Allow them to dry.
4. Apply as many coats of gesso as are necessary to fill any cracks or nicks, or to produce the desired thickness. Allow this to dry.
5. Sandpaper the plate until smooth.
6. Paint the entire plate with a base color.
7. Decorations can now be added with contrasting colors.
8. Apply a protective coat of varnish, shellac, or plastic spray over the plate if tempera paint is used. Use sprays with optimum ventilation.

linear string

procedure

1. Make pencil drawing of the desired subject.
2. Cover the pencil drawing with wax paper and fasten it in place with tape.
3. Place glue-covered string on wax paper over the line drawing.
4. When glue is dry, remove the string construction from the wax paper.

Note: If color is wanted, the string can be dyed before or painted after the design is completed. These objects can be incorporated into mobiles.

supplies

1. Heavy string or cord
2. Wax paper
3. Glue
4. Pencil
5. Paper
6. Tape

liquid solder ornaments

procedure

1. Draw design with felt tip pen on breakable hollow shape. If balloon is used, inflate to desired size and tie the end.
2. With a firm pressure on the tube of liquid solder, follow felt tip pen lines.
3. Stop squeezing tube just before crossing or meeting another line. Solder tends to spread when two wet lines meet.
4. When design is completely covered with liquid solder, allow to dry. Repeat the same process over the first design at least two more times. Continue to use the same precautions.
5. When completely dry, break the hollow form over a paper bag or waste-basket to catch the numerous chips that result.
6. Gently smooth any rough edges with tweezers.
7. Spray ornament with desired color.

Note: Flat designs, as in the following illustrations, can be created on wax paper with liquid solder. Peel away the wax paper when the design is hard. Turn the design over and draw a line of solder over the first design.

A handle can be made by either covering the lower half of the shape with a design and adding several lines of solder over the top which are connected to each side of the design, or by drawing several straight lines of solder on wax paper which can be peeled off when hard and attached to the sides of the basket with a dab of solder.

supplies

1. Thin, breakable, hollow glass Christmas ornament, small balloon, egg shell (blown) (See page 224.)
2. Liquid solder
3. Felt tip pen
4. Wax paper
5. Tweezers
6. Spray paint

mailing tube containers

This project can be used to make banks, napkin rings, pencil and brush holders, planters, bracelets (see page 28).

procedure

1. If a base is needed, place a piece of cardboard under the end of the tube, trace around it, cut it, and affix the base to the mailing tube with the polymer or glue.
2. Paint the surface of the tube with polymer or diluted glue.
3. Tear pieces of the tissue paper and press them on the surface of the tube, or use printed photo as on page 147.
4. Continue with layers of glue and paper until the desired degree of richness is achieved.
5. Spray surface for protection. Use sprays with optimum ventilation.

Notes: If a bank is desired, cut the top as the base, cut in half, cut out the coin slit, then glue together on the top (Ill. 1).

If a pencil and brush holder is desired, cut the top, and drill holes in the top before gluing to the tube (Ill. 2).

The object can be further decorated with wrapped string, transfer pictures (see page 70), or decorative paper strips (Ill. 3). The interior may also be lined with felt.

Small rings can be used for napkin rings with decoration added (Ill. 4).

If designed as a planter, line the inside with liquid asphaltum to waterproof before use (Ill. 5).

supplies

1. Mailing tube sections
2. Cardboard
3. Colored tissue paper or printed material (see pages 137 and 147)
4. Large watercolor brushes
5. Polymer or white glue and water (equal proportions)
6. Clear spray

mosaic plaster plaque

supplies

1. Cardboard container to be used as a mold
2. Scraps of thin colored or textured linoleum, or thin plastic floor tile
3. Molding plaster
4. Bowl in which to mix plaster
5. Heavyduty scissors
6. Paste
7. Pliers

procedure

1. Place the container, which is to be used as a mold, on a sheet of paper and trace around it with a pencil. This will provide a pictorial area of the same dimensions as the completed work, on which the preliminary drawing may be done. Divide the subject matter in the drawing into interesting sections that can be easily cut from the linoleum or plastic tile.
2. Transfer the various parts of the design to the linoleum or floor tile of the desired color and cut out with scissors. Break into pieces with the pliers if brittle plastic is used.
3. Place a small spot of paste on the face of each piece and fasten face down in the cardboard mold to form the original design. Approximately one-eighth of an inch space should remain between the various sections and the edge of the mold.
4. Mix the plaster as follows (see illustrations, page 53):

   a. Pour the desired amount of water in the mixing container.
   b. Add the plaster to the water by sifting it through the fingers or gently shaking it from a can or small cup.
   c. Continue adding the sifted plaster to the water until the plaster builds up above the surface.
   d. Stir the plaster thoroughly with the hands until it is smooth and creamy, making sure that any lumps of plaster are broken. Stir gently to avoid bubbles.
   e. Once the plaster is mixed, do not add more water to thin or more plaster to thicken because the same consistency cannot be regained.

   Note: Warming the linoleum will make it easier to cut.

5. Pour the plaster into the mold to the desired thickness. Agitate the box gently to make sure the plaster completely surrounds the individual pieces of the design and to also bring any bubbles to the surface. A wire hook can be placed in the plaster before it hardens completely if a wall plaque is desired.

Note: Begin to clean up immediately after pouring the plaster in the mold—it will harden rapidly once the chemical reaction takes place. Any excess plaster remaining should be wiped from the pan immediately and rolled in newspaper so that it might be disposed of more easily. Do not wash plaster down any drain. When cleaning the hands, tools, and mixing pan, be sure the water runs continuously.

6. Allow the plaster to dry thoroughly before removing the cardboard box mold. If the cardboard adheres to the plaster, wash it off under running water.
7. Smooth any of the sharp edges by scraping with any available tool. Repair any flaws that might appear at this time.
8. The finished plaque can be soaked in a solution of white soap flakes and then wiped dry with a cloth. This will produce a glossy, high-polish finish.

Note: A plaster relief can be created by carefully lifting out the pieces of plastic tile or linoleum.

papier-mâché bowl

supplies

1. Newspapers, paper toweling, or any absorbent paper
2. Scissors or paper cutter
3. Paste thinned to the consistency of cream (wheat paste, library paste, modeling paste, etc.)
4. Container for mixing paste
5. A smooth bowl to be used as a mold. The bowl should also have a small base and a wide mouth with no undercuts.
6. Vaseline, grease, or cream
7. Sandpaper
8. Paint (tempera, enamel, oil paint, etc.)
9. Brush
10. Clear plastic spray, shellac or varnish for protective finish if tempera paint is used
11. Asphaltum to waterproof bowl

procedure

1. Cover the outside surface of the bowl with a film of cream, Vaseline, or grease. This will keep the papier-mâché from sticking to the bowl.
2. Place the bowl upside down on newspaper or cardboard.
3. Cut newspaper or paper toweling into strips, approximately one-half of an inch wide.
4. Mix the paste in a bowl or pan to the consistency of cream.
5. Place a strip of paper into the paste until it is saturated. Remove the strip from the bowl and wipe off the excess paste by pulling it between the fingers.
6. Apply the paste saturated strips directly on the oiled surface of the bowl. One or two layers of strips of just wet paper applied directly to the bowl before applying the paste saturated strips will serve the same purpose as greasing bowl.
7. Continue to apply strips until the entire bowl is covered. Repeat until at least six layers of paper strips are applied. The number of layers can be readily counted if a different kind or color of paper is used for each layer. The strength of the finished bowl will be much greater if each layer of strips is applied in a different direction. Also, make sure that all wrinkles and bubbles are removed after each strip is added.
8. Allow the papier-mâché to dry thoroughly before removing the bowl.
9. Trim the edges of the bowl and apply additional strips to strengthen and smooth the edges. Other imperfections can be repaired at this time.
10. When thoroughly dry, sandpaper the surface until smooth and then decorate.
11. If tempera paint is used for decoration, the surface should be sprayed with clear plastic or painted with shellac or varnish for permanence.
12. Asphaltum painted on the inside of the bowl will waterproof the container.

papier-mâché jewelry

procedure

1. Shape a piece of styrofoam to correspond identically to the desired piece of jewelry.
2. Cut newspaper or paper toweling into strips, approximately one-fourth of an inch wide.
3. Mix the paste in a bowl or pan to the consistency of cream.
4. Immerse a strip of paper into the paste until it is saturated. Remove the strip from the bowl and wipe off the excess paste by pulling it between the fingers.
5. Apply the strips directly to the styrofoam.
6. Continue to apply strips until the entire piece of jewelry is covered. Repeat until several layers of paper strips are applied. The number of layers can be readily counted if a different kind or color of paper is used for each layer. Make sure that all wrinkles and bubbles are removed after each strip is added.
7. Add any desired particular features. This can be done either with papier-mâché or by adding other materials.
8. Allow the papier-mâché to dry thoroughly.
9. Sandpaper the surface until smooth and then decorate.
10. If tempera paint is used for decoration, the surface should be sprayed with clear plastic or painted with shellac or varnish for permanence.
11. Fasten earring or pin back to the back of dry papier-mâché jewelry using glue mixed with a small piece of cotton.

supplies

1. Small pieces of styrofoam
2. Newspapers, paper toweling, or any absorbent paper
3. Scissors or paper cutter
4. Paste thinned to consistency of cream (wheat paste, modeling paste, library paste)
5. Container for mixing paste
6. Sandpaper
7. Paint (tempera, enamel, latex, etc.)
8. Brush
9. Clear plastic spray, shellac, or varnish for protecting finish, if tempera paint is used
10. Glue
11. Jewelry findings (pin and/or earring backs)

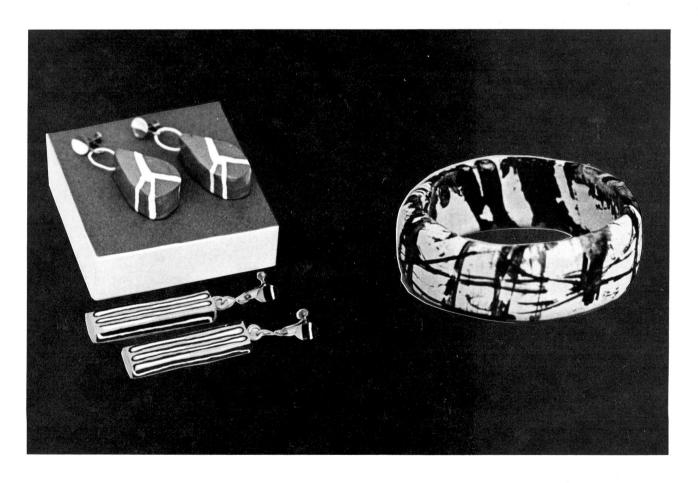

papier-mâché maraca

supplies

1. Newspapers, paper toweling, or any absorbent paper
2. Scissors or paper cutter
3. Paste thinned to consistency of cream (wheat paste, library paste, modeling paste)
4. Container for mixing paste
5. Bottle on which to build form
6. Sandpaper
7. Paint (tempera, latex, enamel, etc.)
8. Brush
9. Clear plastic spray, shellac, or varnish, for protecting finish if tempera paint is used

procedure

1. Cover the surface of the light bulb with a film of cream, vaseline, or grease. This will keep the papier-mâché from sticking to the bulb.
2. Cut newspaper or paper toweling into strips, approximately one-half of an inch wide.
3. Mix the paste in a bowl or pan to the consistency of cream.
4. Place a strip of paper into the paste until it is saturated. Remove the strip from the bowl and wipe off the excess paste by pulling it between the fingers.
5. Apply the paste-saturated strip directly to the oiled surface of the light bulb.
6. Continue to apply strips until the entire bulb is covered. Repeat until at least six layers of paper strips are applied. The number of layers can be readily counted if a different kind or color of paper is used for each layer. The strength of the finished maraca will be much greater if each strip is applied in a different direction. Also, make sure that all wrinkles and bubbles are removed after each strip is added.
7. Place the maraca on a crumpled piece of newspaper, and allow to dry thoroughly. The crumpled paper allows the air to circulate around the maraca.
8. When completely dry, rap the maraca sharply against the floor, wall, or radiator to break the bulb inside the paper covering. The broken pieces of glass provide the sound when shaken. If a hole is punctured, it is easily repaired with the addition of more strips.
9. Sandpaper the surface until smooth and then decorate.
10. If tempera paint is used for decoration, the surface should then be sprayed with clear plastic or painted with shellac or varnish for permanence.

papier-mâché over balloon

procedure

1. Cut newspaper or paper toweling into strips, approximately one-half of an inch wide.
2. Mix the paste in a bowl or pan to the consistency of cream.
3. Inflate the balloon to the desired size and tie it closed.
4. Place a strip of paper in the paste until it is saturated. Remove the strip from the bowl and wipe off the excess paste by pulling it between the fingers.
5. Apply the paste saturated strip directly to the balloon.
6. Continue to apply strips until the entire balloon is covered. Repeat until at least six layers of paper strips are applied. The number of layers can be readily counted if a different kind or color of paper is used for each layer. The strength of the finished balloon will be much greater if each strip is applied in a different direction. Also, make sure that all wrinkles and bubbles are removed after each strip is added.

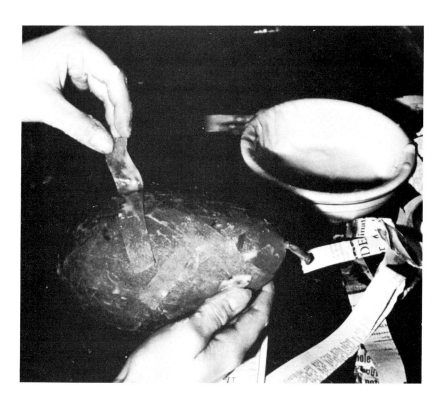

7. Allow papier-mâché to dry thoroughly.
8. A number of different and interesting objects can be created at this point.

   a. An opening can be cut into an egg shape and an Easter egg crèche can be built inside.
   b. A perfect sphere can be used as a globe for the geography class. The continents can be painted, built up with papier-mâché, or built in relief with a salt and flour mixture (see page 60).

(see page 60)

supplies

1. Newspapers, paper toweling, or any absorbent paper
2. Scissors or paper cutter
3. Paste thinned to the consistency of cream (wheat paste, library paste, modeling paste)
4. Container for mixing paste
5. Balloon
6. Sandpaper
7. Paint (tempera, enamel, oil paint, etc.)
8. Brush
9. Clear plastic spray, shellac, or varnish for protective finish if tempera paint is used

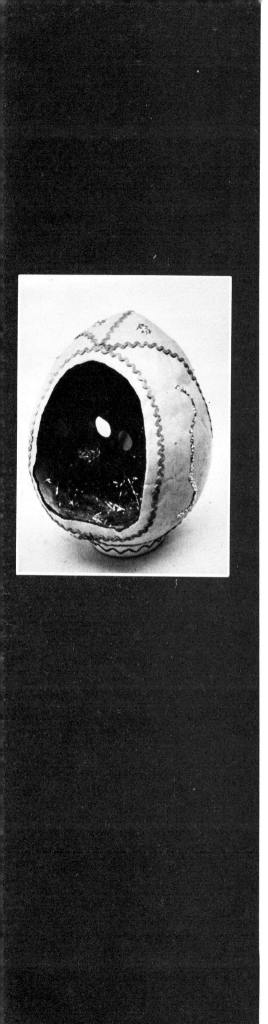

c. When cut in half, the balloon shape can be used as a foundation for two masks, two bowls, or one of each. If a mask is desired, openings can be cut for the eyes, and features added with either papier-mâché or by fastening other materials in place (yarn for hair, kernels of corn for teeth, cut paper for ears, etc.)

d. The shape of the papier-mâché balloon might suggest an animal, bird, fish, etc. Its particular features can be applied with papier-mâché or by fastening other material to the form.

9. Sandpaper the surface of any of the above objects before decorating.
10. If tempera paint is used for decoration, the surface should be sprayed with clear plastic or painted with shellac or varnish for permanence. Use sprays with optimum ventilation.

papier-mâché over bottle

procedure

1. Cut newspaper or paper toweling into strips, approximately one-half of an inch wide.
2. Mix the paste in a bowl or pan to the consistency of cream.
3. Submerge a strip of paper in the paste until it is saturated. Remove the strip from the bowl and wipe off the excess paste by pulling the strip between the fingers.
4. Apply the paste-saturated strip directly to the bottle.
5. Continue to apply strips until the entire bottle is covered. Repeat until at least six layers of paper strips are applied. The number of layers can be readily counted if a different kind or color of paper is used for each layer. The strength of the finished piece will be much greater if each strip is applied in a different direction. Also, make sure that all wrinkles and bubbles are removed after each strip is added.
6. Place the bottle on a crumpled piece of paper and allow it to dry thoroughly. The crumpled paper allows the air to circulate around the piece.
7. When the papier-mâché over the bottle is dry, the surface can be decorated with a choice of three-dimensional materials that are held in position with paste covered strips.
8. When dry, sandpaper the surface until smooth and then decorate.
9. If tempera paint is used for decoration, the surface should be sprayed with clear plastic or painted with shellac or varnish for permanence. Use sprays with optimum ventilation.

supplies

1. Newspapers, paper toweling, or any absorbent paper
2. Scissors or paper cutter
3. Paste thinned to consistency of cream (wheat paste, library paste, modeling paste)
4. Container for mixing paste
5. Bottle on which to build form
6. Sandpaper
7. Paint (tempera, latex, enamel, etc.)
8. Brush
9. Clear plastic spray, shellac, or varnish, for protecting finish if tempera paint is used

papier-mâché over frame

supplies

1. Window screen, chicken wire, wire, paper, mailing tubes, sticks, etc. (to be used individually or collectively to form the general shape of the object to be covered with papier-mâché)
2. Wire, nails, gummed paper, glue, etc., for use in fastening the frame together
3. Newspapers, paper toweling, or any absorbent paper
4. Scissors, or paper cutter
5. Paste thinned to the consistency of cream (wheat paste, library paste, modeling paste)
6. Container for mixing paste
7. Sandpaper
8. Paint (tempera, enamel, oil paint, etc.)
9. Brush
10. Clear plastic spray, shellac, or varnish for protecting finish if tempera paint is used

procedure

1. Build a frame or armature to the general shape of the chosen subject. Fasten the various parts of the skeleton together securely, using the wire, nails, tape, or appropriate material.
2. Cut newspaper or paper toweling into strips, approximately one-half of an inch wide.
3. Mix the paste in a bowl or pan to the consistency of cream.
4. Place a strip of paper in the paste until it is saturated. Remove the strip from the bowl and wipe off the excess paste by pulling the strip between the fingers.
5. Apply the strips directly over the frame.
6. Continue to apply strips until the entire frame is covered. Repeat until at least six layers of paper strips are applied. The number of layers can be readily counted if a different kind or color of paper is used for each layer. The strength of the finished frame will be much greater if each strip is applied in a different direction. Also, make sure that all wrinkles and bubbles are removed after each strip is added.
7. Add any particular features not incorporated in the original skeleton. This can be done either with papier-mâché or by adding other materials.
8. Allow the papier-mâché to dry thoroughly.
9. Sandpaper the surface until smooth and then decorate.
10. If tempera paint is used for decoration, the surface should be sprayed with clear plastic or painted with shellac or varnish for permanence. Use sprays with optimum ventilation.
11. Additional materials such as yarn for hair, buttons for eyes, etc., can be added to further enhance the finished product.

papier-mâché pulp objects

procedure

1. Tear (do not cut with cutter or scissors) paper into small pieces no bigger than one-half inch square. Be sure edges of pieces are ragged.
2. Place the torn paper in a container and cover with water, and at the same time, stir to make sure all the paper becomes wet.
3. Add a teaspoonful of salt for each quart of mixture to prevent spoilage. Allow to soak for at least thirty-six hours.
4. Mix and squeeze the mixture until it becomes pulp.
5. Mix in wallpaper paste in small amounts as needed.
6. Model the forms with the mixture.
7. Allow the pulp to dry thoroughly.
8. Sandpaper the surface until smooth and then decorate.
9. If tempera paint is used for decoration, the surface should be sprayed with clear plastic or painted with shellac or varnish for permanence. Use sprays with optimum ventilation.

Note: Papier-mâché pulp can be used for dishes, plaques, ornaments, puppets, marionettes, maps, etc.

supplies

1. Newspaper, or tissue, or paper towels
2. Wallpaper paste or modeling paste
3. Table salt
4. Container

papier-mâché puppet head

procedure

1. Create a puppet head and neck with the plastic clay. The neck will eventually serve two purposes: first, a place to fasten clothing and secondly, a place for the middle finger to control the puppet. When forming the head, exaggerate the features as the thickness of the applied paper strips tends to reduce feature recognition.
2. Cut newspaper or paper toweling into strips, approximately one-half of an inch wide.
3. Mix the paste in a bowl or pan to the consistency of cream.

supplies

1. Newspapers, paper toweling, or any absorbent paper
2. Scissors or paper cutter
3. Paste thinned to the consistency of cream (wheat paste, library paste, modeling paste)
4. Container for mixing paste

5. Plastic clay
6. Sandpaper
7. Knife, saw, or single-edge razor blade
8. Paint (tempera, enamel, oil paint, etc.)
9. Brush
10. Clear plastic spray, shellac, or varnish for protective finish if tempera paint is used

4. Place a strip of paper into the paste until it is saturated. Remove the strip from the bowl and wipe off the excess paste by pulling the strip between the fingers.
5. Apply the paste saturated strip directly to the puppet head.
6. Continue to apply strips until the entire head is covered. Repeat until at least six layers of paper strips are applied. The number of layers can be readily counted if a different kind or color of paper is used for each layer. The strength of the finished puppet will be much greater if each strip is applied in a different direction. Also, make sure that all wrinkles and bubbles are removed after each strip is added.
7. Place the puppet head on a crumpled piece of paper and allow it to dry thoroughly. The crumpled paper allows the air to circulate around the puppet head.
8. When the puppet head is dry, cut it in half with a sharp knife or saw and remove the clay (Ill. 1).
9. Place the two halves together and fasten with additional strips. It may also be necessary to apply several strips over the bottom edge of the neck for strength.
10. When thoroughly dry, sandpaper until smooth, and then decorate (Ill. 2).
11. If tempera paint is used for decoration, the surface should be sprayed with clear plastic, or painted with shellac or varnish for permanence. Use sprays with optimum ventilation.
12. Additional material such as yarn for hair, buttons for eyes, etc., can be added to further enhance the finished product (Ill. 3).

1

2

3

pariscraft figures

procedure

1. Roll up the cardboard to produce a cone. Staple or glue the ends together. Cut off the point.
2. Tear off a piece of cotton the size desired for the head.
3. Cut Pariscraft into small strips, which can be dampened and wrapped around the cotton ball.
4. When dry, glue the head on the narrow end of the cone.
5. Cut fairly long strips of Pariscraft to a width suitable for arms and roll them up until the desired arm thickness is achieved. Cut the roll in half and dampen.
6. Glue the arms to the cone (body).
7. Glue the pieces of yarn to the head, building it up to simulate hair. If desired, the yarn may first be dipped in wheat paste, in which case the glue is unnecessary.
8. Paint the face, its features, and the arms.
9. Produce the desired clothed effect by painting and/or gluing material to the body.

Note: This procedure describes a method of making small figures; experimentation will reveal many other possibilities.

supplies

1. A piece of cardboard, to be used as a body, cut according to the desired size (a tube may be used)
2. Yarn, to be used as hair
3. Assorted fabrics
4. Glue
5. Cotton
6. Paints (acrylic recommended, tempera suitable)
7. Wheat paste (optional)
8. Pariscraft (fabric, in roll, with preapplied coating of plaster)

peep box

supplies

1. Cardboard box (shoe box, hat box, etc.)
2. Scissors
3. Rubber cement, paste, glue, or stapler
4. Tempera paint, watercolors, crayons, colored chalks, or color inks
5. Paint brush and water jar, if paints are used
6. Assorted papers
7. A variety of materials to be used for decorative purposes: cloth, felt, ribbon, yarn, dried coffee grounds, buttons, clay, salt and flour mixture, twigs, pebbles, etc. These materials can be determined more easily after the subject for the peep box has been decided upon.

procedure

As in the shadowbox (page 65), the procedure for this project will vary somewhat, depending upon the type of peep box to be made. Scenes from children's stories, poems, or songs may be depicted in the peep boxes. It is possible, too, to create make-believe aquariums (suspend the fish, etc., from a string and use colored cellophane over the top and face of the box to give the illusion of water). Peep boxes can also be very effective as Christmas crèches and puppet theaters.

1. Cut a small spy hole opening in one end of a box. In some cases an opening at each end is advisable.
2. Cut a number of openings or doors in the lid in order to allow light in the box. These openings can be placed strategically to allow spotlighting. Light can be controlled in the box by opening or closing the "doors" in the lid.
3. Design the sides of the box. Any one of a number of techniques may be used for this: potato print, crayon engraving, chalk stencil, colored paper, finger paint, watercolor, etc. A combination of several of these techniques will make an interesting peep box.
4. Many methods are available for making trees, houses, barns, figures, etc. Cleansing tissue can be modeled as the foliage for trees. It may be tinted with colored inks or tempera paint. Twigs, match sticks, and paper cylinders can serve as the trunks of the tree. Bits of sponges also make suitable foliage when painted. One may choose to use paper sculpture as a method of making trees, shrubs, etc.

   Houses, barns, and other buildings can be made from tiny boxes, corrugated cardboard, or paper sculpture. These, too, may be painted with colored inks or tempera paints.

   Figures and animals can be made from wire, pipe cleaners, clay, salt and flour mixture, papier-mâché, clothespins, etc.

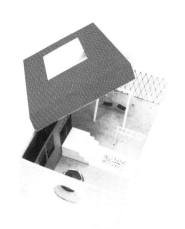

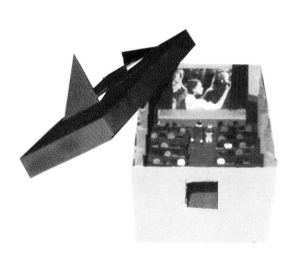

pipe cleaner figures

supplies

1. White or colored pipe cleaners
2. Any cutting tool that can be used to cut the pipe cleaners to the desired length

procedure

1. Interesting stick figures can be created by bending and twisting the pipe cleaners.
2. Form and thickness can be added to the stick figures by wrapping additional pipe cleaners around the body, arms, and legs, etc.

Note: These figures may be used in shadowboxes, sand table displays, small stage sets, or for individual party favors or decorations.

plaster mixing

procedure

Mix the plaster as follows:

1. Pour the desired amount of water into the mixing container (Ill. 1).
2. Add the plaster to the water by sifting it through the fingers or gently shaking it from a can or small cup (Ill. 2).
3. Continue adding the sifted plaster to the water until the plaster builds up above the surface. Allow to soak twenty or thirty seconds to thoroughly blend the mixture (Ill. 3).
4. Stir the plaster thoroughly with the hands until it is smooth and creamy, making sure that any lumps of plaster are broken, and stir gently to avoid bubbles (Ill. 4).
5. Once the plaster is mixed do not add more water to thin, or more plaster to thicken, because the same consistency cannot be regained.
6. Pour the plaster into a container, which can be used for the mold. Agitate the mold gently to bring any bubbles to the surface (Ill. 5).

Note: Begin to clean up immediately after pouring the plaster in the mold— it will harden rapidly once the chemical reaction takes place. Any excess plaster remaining should be wiped from the pan immediately and rolled in newspaper so that it might be disposed of more easily. Do not wash plaster down any drain. When cleaning the hands, tools, and mixing pan, be sure the water runs continuously.

supplies

1. Molding plaster
2. Container for mixing plaster
3. Water
4. Newspaper for cleaning
5. Container to be used as mold

1

2

3

4

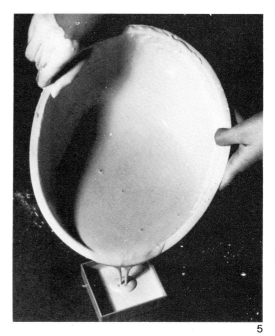

5

plaster space forms

supplies

1. Plaster
2. Small balloon
3. Yarn
4. Bowl for mixing plaster
5. Can of spray paint, if color is desired

procedure

1. Inflate the balloon and tie the end closed.
2. Mix plaster as follows (see illustrations page 53):

   a. Pour the desired amount of water in the mixing container.
   b. Add the plaster to the water by sifting it through the fingers or gently shaking it from a can or small cup.
   c. Continue adding the sifted plaster to the water until the plaster builds up above the surface.
   d. Stir the plaster thoroughly with the hands until it is smooth and creamy, making sure that any lumps of plaster are broken and stir gently to avoid bubbles.
   e. Once the plaster is mixed do not add more water to thin, or more plaster to thicken, because the same consistency cannot be regained.

3. Holding one end of the yarn, immerse it in the plaster (if the yarn is too fine, use a double or triple strand). Pull the yarn from the bowl and through the fingers of one hand, wiping off the excess plaster.
4. Place the plaster saturated yarn on the inflated balloon in a decorative manner, making sure the yarn crosses over itself frequently.

Note: Begin to clean up when the plaster begins to thicken—it will harden rapidly once the chemical reaction takes place. Any excess plaster remaining should be wiped from the pan immediately and rolled in newspaper so that it might be disposed of more easily. Do not wash plaster down any drain. When cleaning hands, tools, and mixing pan, be sure the water runs continuously.

5. Allow the plaster to harden and dry thoroughly before puncturing the balloon.
6. Hold the plaster decorated balloon in a wastebasket or large cardboard box to catch the numerous plaster chips that result when the balloon is punctured.
7. Gently smooth any rough edges and paint the plaster. Spray paint will work best. Painting before the balloon is punctured will leave the inside pure white.
8. Additional decoration of various materials can be placed inside the space form.

plaster tile mosaic

procedure

1. Place the wood or masonite to be used as the tile on a sheet of paper and trace around it with a pencil. This will provide a pictorial area the same dimensions as the completed tile.
2. Create a drawing within this area.
3. Transfer the drawing to the wood or masonite.
4. Break the plastic into small pieces with the pliers and glue in place on the tile. Allow a small space between each piece as it is placed. If pieces are too small they can be picked up with tweezers.

   a. Avoid light-colored tiles as they will not contrast with the white plaster surrounding each piece.
   b. If the entire tile is not to be covered with mosaic, be sure a border is included.

5. Mix the plaster as follows (see illustrations, page 53):

   a. Pour the desired amount of water into the mixing container.
   b. Add the plaster to the water by sifting it through the fingers or gently shaking it from a can or small cup.
   c. Continue adding the sifted plaster to the water until the plaster builds up above the surface of the water.
   d. Stir the plaster thoroughly with the hands until it is smooth and creamy. Make sure any lumps of plaster are broken and also stir gently to avoid creating bubbles.
   e. Once the plaster is mixed, do not add any more water to thin, or more plaster to thicken, because the same consistency cannot be regained.

6. Pour the plaster over the tile which has been placed on newspaper and work it between the mosaic pieces.

Note: Begin to clean up immediately after pouring the plaster into the mold—it will harden rapidly once the chemical reaction takes place. Any excess plaster remaining should be wiped from the pan immediately and rolled in newspaper so that it might be disposed of more easily. Do not wash plaster down any drain. When cleaning the hands, tools, and mixing pan, be sure the water runs continuously.

7. Level the plaster by pulling the straightedge over the surface. (Thin pieces of mosaic should be used, as thick pieces will be pulled out of place.)
8. Fill in all bubbles and repair any flaws before the plaster becomes too hard.
9. Only a thin film of plaster should appear on the mosaic tiles after scraping with the straightedge.
10. When almost dry, clean film from the tile pieces with fingers, tissue, or rag.

supplies

1. Piece of wood or masonite the size of the mosaic to be made
2. Scraps of thin colored plastic floor tile (all must be the same thickness)
3. Molding plaster
4. Bowl in which to mix plaster
5. Pliers
6. Glue
7. Straightedge wider and longer than the tile to be made
8. Tweezers

procedure

1. Cut empty container in half—each piece will serve as a mask. If possible, have the containers cut in half with a power band saw. Observe all safety precautions in using cutting tools.
2. Cut out any openings necessary for eyes, nose, or mouth.
3. Additions can be added with pieces cut from the bottle or paper, paint, and pipe cleaners.
4. Staple an elastic band to each side of the mask to hold it to the head comfortably.

Note: Empty containers can also be used for carryalls, planters, and bird feeders. If planter is to be made from plastic container, stones should be placed in the bottom for drainage. Decoration can be added to the bird feeder with adhesive paper or paint.

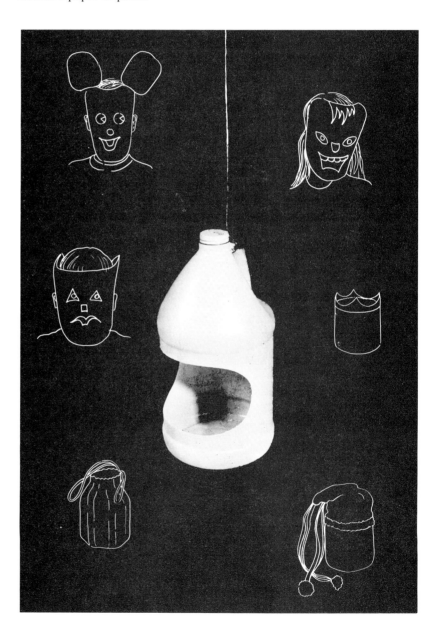

pressed nature notepaper

procedure

1. Collect flowers, ferns, leaves, grasses, etc., and dry them by pressing between sheets of newspaper weighted with books or other heavy objects. Let them dry about one week, changing newspapers occasionally.
2. Arrange these natural objects where they appear to be most pleasing on the notepaper or place cards.
3. When satisfied with the arrangement, glue into place by dotting the backs of the leaves, flowers, etc., with glue, just enough to hold them in place until the Contact paper can be applied.
4. Cut a square or rectangle of clear Contact paper large enough to cover and extend a little beyond the design.
5. Peel the backing from the Contact paper and carefully apply it, pressing it firmly to the place card or notepaper. If a bubble forms in the Contact paper, prick it with a pin and press it out.

supplies

1. Notepaper or place cards
2. Leaves, delicate flowers, lacy ferns, grasses, etc.
3. Newspapers
4. Glue
5. Clear Contact paper
6. Ruler
7. Scissors

pressed nature picture

supplies

1. Leaves, delicate flowers, lacy ferns, grasses, etc.
2. Newspapers
3. Matboard and cardboard the same size for backing
4. White or light-colored material (material used for drapery or dress linings is good)
5. Scissors
6. Ruler
7. Pencil
8. Razor blade
9. Glue
10. Decorative braids (optional)
11. Material to cover top mat (tiny checks or prints might enhance picture)
12. Inexpensive picture frame
13. Double-edged tape, if mat is to be covered with material

procedure

1. Collect flowers, leaves, ferns, grasses, etc., and dry them by pressing between sheets of newspaper weighted with books or other heavy objects. Let dry about one week, changing newspapers occasionally.
2. Follow steps one through nine on pages 103 and 104. "Cutting a Mat," to determine the size of the finished picture.
3. White or light plain material may be stretched over the cardboard covering an area an inch larger all around than the opening of the mat.
4. Arrange dry, pressed flowers, leaves, etc., into a pleasing design, and when satisfied, glue them into place. (Just dot the backs of leaves, flowers, etc., with glue as they are pressed into place on the picture.)
5. The top mat of the picture may be covered with decorative material if desired. Stretch and turn the under-edge of the material and hold it in place with double-edged tape. The inside corners of the material will need to be slit in order to turn and tape. Simple, decorative braids, outlining the inside edge of mat, may enhance picture. It is necessary to experiment to obtain best results.
6. Frame the finished picture. (Frames may be spray painted, stained, or rubbed with gold paint and then buffed.) Use sprays with optimum ventilation.

relief mosaic from seeds or beads

procedure

1. Sketch the design on construction paper, carefully defining the areas where seeds are to be placed.
2. Using glue, mount the construction paper on cardboard, the same size as the construction paper.
3. Spread the glue on one area of the design at a time and press the seeds, beads, or natural objects into place, filling the area. (For a neater appearance in the design, it is best to outline each area, then proceed to fill the rest of the area.)
4. When placing small pieces, it is helpful to put a dab of glue on the end of a toothpick to pick up and place each seed.
5. When glue is completely dry and excess pieces have been shaken off, spray the design with three thin coats of clear spray.

Note: Additional details may be added to the picture with heavy string, yarn, or other decorative materials (for whiskers, stems, etc.).

supplies

1. Cardboard
2. Construction paper
3. White glue
4. Assortment of seeds or natural objects
5. Food coloring
6. Pencil
7. String or yarn
8. Clear spray

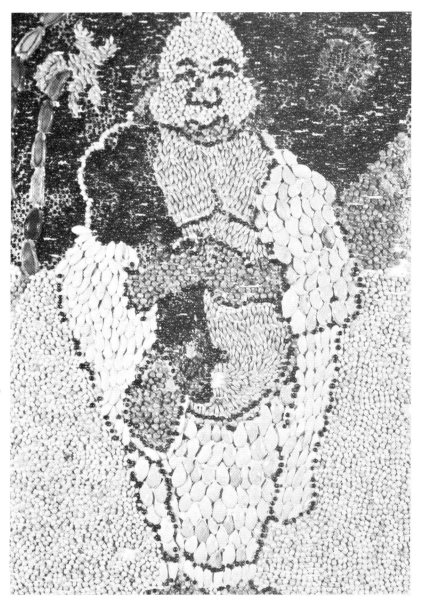

salt and flour relief

supplies

1. Combine three parts salt with one part flour, and enough water to bring solution to the consistency of dough. This will create a mass suitable for sculptural modeling; the thickness may be modified for individual needs or desired methods of application by varying the quantity of water.
2. Heavy cardboard or piece of wood
3. Watercolor paints
4. Brush
5. Water container

procedure

1. Cover the cardboard or wood with a thin film of salt and flour mixture.
2. Keeping a design in mind, create a semiround relief, building up masses of the salt and flour mixture to various heights. Additional salt and flour may be added when the first application has dried enough to support another layer.
3. When the modeling is completed, it may be embellished by the addition of color while still moist.
4. Additional interest may be created by pressing objects, textures, and patterns into the wet salt and flour.

Note: Topographical maps or aerial views are especially suitable for treatment in this manner.

sand candles

procedure

1. Pack damp sand into a box or bucket (Ill. 1).
2. Hollow the shape of the candle in the damp sand. These shapes can be created with your hands, a bottle, pencils, sticks, or any type of tool that can be pressed into the sand to make a hollow.
3. Place a wick into the mold by tying one end to a stick suspended across the top of the mold (Ill. 2). On the other end, tie a weight and drop into the hollow. Make sure the wick is centered and stretched tight. A candle itself may be inserted to form the wick.
4. Melt the wax in a double boiler to a temperature of 190° to 230°F. or 88°C to 210°C (standard pouring temperature). Use a thermometer to make sure, for wax reaches a flash point at approximately 400°F, or 204°C.
5. Add colored crayons to the melted wax to reach desired color.
6. Grip the container of melted wax with gloves or hot pad and pour melted wax into moist sand mold (Ill. 3). Different colored wax poured in layers makes interesting effects.
7. Leave wax in sand until completely hard. Wash off excess sand.
8. If bottom of candle is uneven, it can be leveled on a hot surface.

Note: In case of fire, cover flame with a lid or baking soda. Never use water to extinguish the flame.

supplies

1. Wax (old candles work best, but clean and snip off burned wick); paraffin (good and melts rapidly); beeswax (excellent, but too expensive); mutton tallow (good, but becomes rancid too easily). See page 247.
2. Wicks, cotton twine (old candle wicks)
3. Can or old pan, for melting wax
4. Colored crayons, for coloring wax
5. Double boiler
6. Thermometer (candy thermometer)
7. Box or bucket
8. Damp fine sand
9. Gloves, hot pad, or cloth

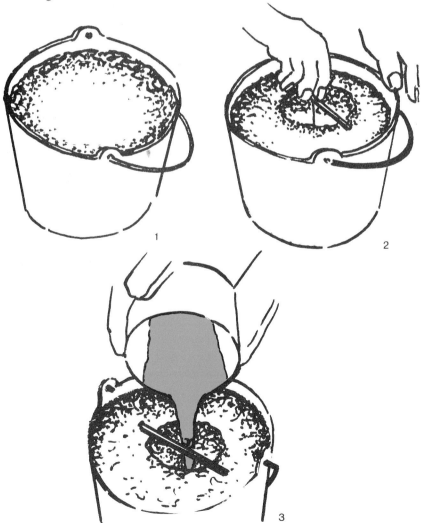

1

2

3

sand painting

supplies

1. Fine sand of various colors
2. Jars or bowls, for mixing and storing the sand
3. Heavy cardboard or piece of wood
4. Paper cone or spoon
5. Varnish, shellac, glue, or paste
6. Watercolor paint
7. Brush

procedure

1. Sketch a design lightly with a pencil on the cardboard or wood.
2. Brush in the background colors in which sand is not desired.
3. Choose the areas to be done in a particular color sand and paint a thin coat of shellac, varnish, glue (thin with water), or paste on these parts (paint a small area at a time).
4. Trickle or sprinkle the colored sand from a paper cone or spoon onto the areas that have been covered with paste, varnish, or shellac.
5. Allow the work to dry for a few minutes, then lift the work and tap it lightly so excess sand is removed.
6. Repeat this process for all additional colors.

Note: American Indians poured sand from the hand along the second joint of the index finger. The thumb was used to stop the flow of sand.

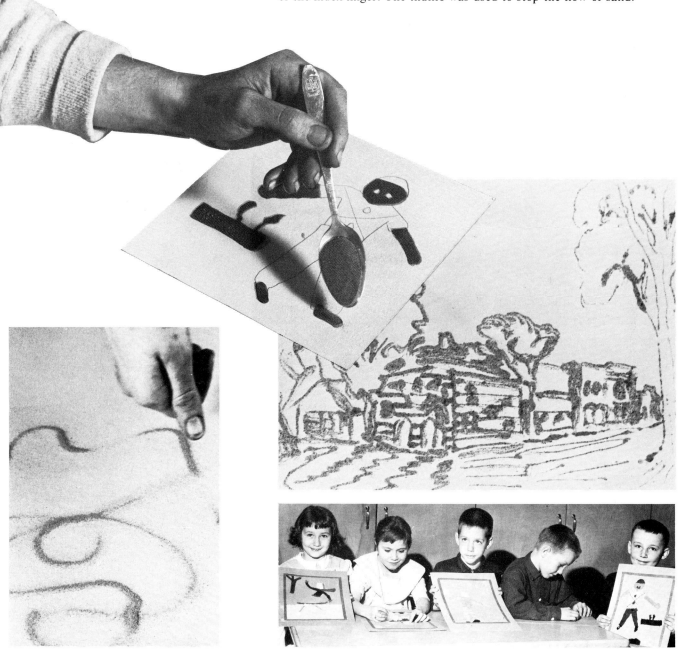

sealed nature pattern

procedure

1. Cut two sheets of wax paper that are of equal size.
2. Lay one sheet flat and arrange the plant life on it to create the desired pattern.
3. Place the other waxed sheet over the first, covering the plant life.
4. Iron over the second sheet with a *warm* flat iron. This will seal the waxed sheets together, preserving the plant life.

Note: Suggested applications for this design are: table runner, bulletin or blackboard frieze, window transparencies, etc. Interesting effects using yarn, string, colored paper, etc., may also be used.

1. Interesting forms of *flat* plant life, such as leaves, weeds, grasses
2. Wax paper
3. Iron

sewn seed jewelry

supplies

1. Variety of dried seeds (corn, beans, cantaloupe, watermelon, grapefruit, apple, pumpkin, tree pods, etc.)
2. Needle
3. Heavy buttonhole cotton thread

procedure

1. After determining the sequence in which the seeds will appear, string the seeds on a predetermined length of thread, making allowance for knots at the ends.
2. Thread the seeds on the thread until there is just room for a triple knot at the end.
3. Tie the knot and, if desired, spray with an acrylic to preserve the seeds.

Notes: Ornamental objects may be spaced between the seeds.
Cold water will soften the seed.
Shell macaroni can also be used. Dip in hot water to soften.

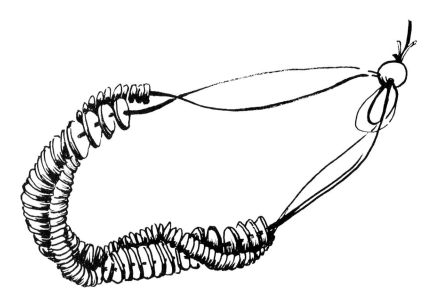

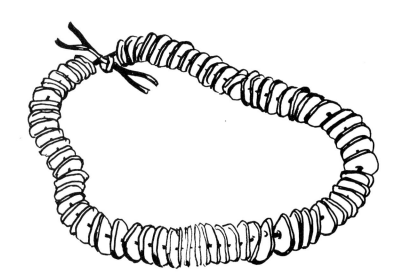

shadowbox

procedure

The procedure for this project will vary somewhat, depending upon the type of shadowbox to be made. Scenes from children's stories, poems, or songs may be depicted in a shadowbox. It is possible, too, to create make-believe aquariums (suspend the fish, etc., from a string and use colored cellophane over the face of the box to give the illusion of water). Shadowboxes can also be very effective as Christmas crèches and puppet theaters.

1. Design the background for the picture. Any one of a number of techniques may be used for this: potato printing, crayon engraving, chalk stenciling, finger painting, watercolor, etc. A combination of several of these techniques will make an interesting background for the shadowbox.
2. Many methods are available for making trees, houses, barns, figures, etc. Cleansing tissue can be modeled into the foliage for trees. It may be tinted with colored inks or tempera paint. Twigs, match sticks, or paper cylinders can serve as the trunks of the tree. Bits of sponges also make suitable foliage when painted. One may choose to use paper sculpture as a method of making trees, shrubs, etc.

   Houses, barns, and other buildings can be made from tiny boxes, corrugated cardboard, or paper sculpture. These, too, may be painted with colored inks or tempera paints.

   Figures and animals can be made from wire, pipe cleaners, clay, the salt and flour mixture, papier-mâché, clothespins, etc.

Note: The possibilities for this project are unlimited.

supplies

1. Cardboard box (shoe box, hat box, etc.)
2. Scissors
3. Rubber cement, paste, glue, or stapler
4. Tempera paint, watercolors, crayons, colored chalks, or color inks
5. Paint brush and water jar, if paints are used
6. Assorted papers
7. A variety of materials to be used for decorative purposes: cloth, felt, ribbon, yarn, dried coffee grounds, buttons, clay, salt and flour mixture, twigs, pebbles, etc. These materials can be determined more easily after the subject for the peep box has been decided upon.

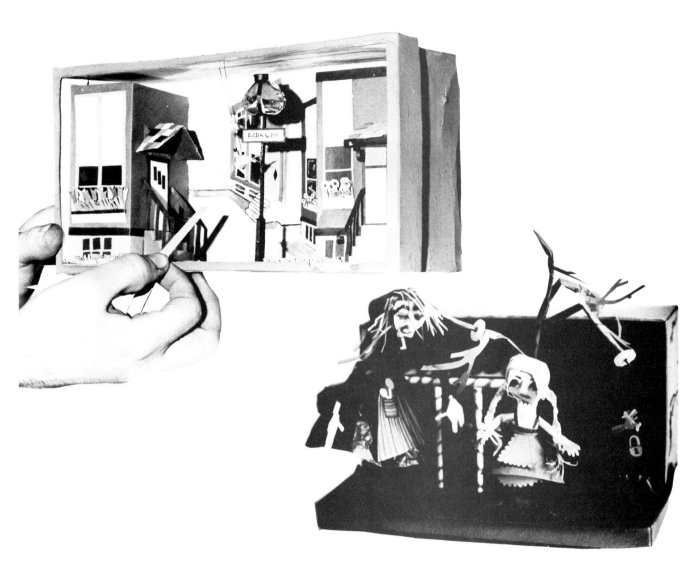

stick construction

procedure

Method A
1. First, cut the wooden pieces for the back and front of the structure. (The hole for a wren house should be one inch in diameter.)
2. Sticks are then glued to the edges of the front and back pieces to enclose the shape.

Method B
1. Various bowls or other constructions can be created by laying sticks on top of one another much like laying bricks. Place a drop of glue where sticks cross one another.
2. Continue process until bowl is built to desired height.

Note: Various combinations of sticks may be used to create figures, creatures, or objects.

supplies

1. Popsicle sticks or tongue depressors
2. Fine sandpaper
3. Glue
4. Enamel spray paint or fast-drying clear finish
5. Wooden pieces for back and front of structure

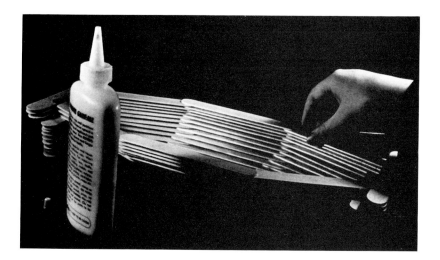

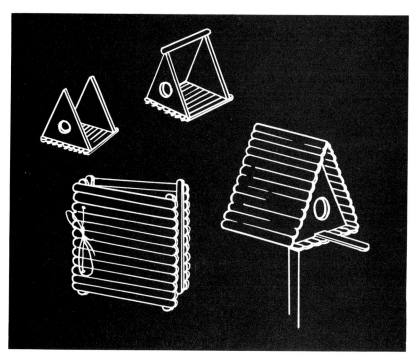

string picture

supplies

1. String or yarn
2. Paper
3. Glue

procedure

1. Make a light pencil drawing on a sheet of paper. Use colored paper if white string is to be used.
2. Coat the string with glue, then place it over the pencil lines.

Note: When using yarn, it may be easier to trail the glue on the drawing and place the yarn on the glue.

string and pin plaques

procedure

1. Decide on size and shape of plaque and cut from a piece of Upsom Board.
2. Cover Upsom Board with a piece of felt or cloth. Pull the cloth over the edges and fasten in back with glue or tape. Be sure cloth is stretched tightly.
3. Push enough straight pins into cloth-covered Upsom Board to form a design. Measure the distance between the pins if the design is to be geometric (Ill. 1).
4. Tie string or thread to one pin, then wind around other pins to form design (Ill. 2).
5. Tie string when one color design is completed. Tie another color string to a pin, and begin to form another part of design.
6. Place hook in back so plaque may be hung.

Note: Individual creative designs may be produced by experimenting with pin placement.

supplies

1. Upsom board, one-half-inch thick
2. Straight pins or finishing nails
3. Assorted colors of thread or string
4. Piece of felt or cloth
5. Tape or glue

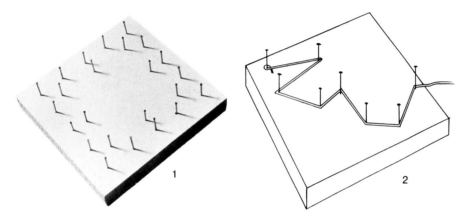

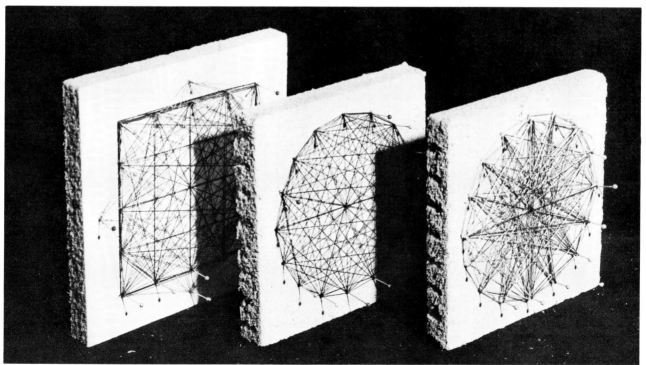

transfer picture

supplies

1. Color photograph printed on high-quality glossy paper
2. Clear polymer medium (painting medium for acrylic paint)
3. Paint brush
4. Tape
5. Wax paper
6. Material or object to which the print is to be transferred
7. Small roller

procedure

1. Tape the photographic print face up on the wax paper (Ill. 1).
2. Paint the print with six or seven coats of clear polymer. Alternate the direction of each coat, allowing ten to fifteen minutes drying time between each coat (Ill. 2).
3. Allow one hour for all of the coats to dry.
4. Soak the coated print in warm, sudsy water until all of the paper can be peeled from the back of the picture (Ill. 3). In some cases the paper may have to be rubbed from the back. The soaking time may take an hour, depending on the thickness of the paper. Be careful not to tear or stretch the remaining film of ink and polymer.
5. Allow the print to dry.
6. Apply the print to any surface by first brushing a coat of clear polymer on the surface. Adhere the print while this coating is wet (Ill. 4).
7. Remove any bubbles by pressing out from the center. If any bubbles persist, puncture them with a pin.

Note: With proper mounting on clear acetate or plastic, the transfer photographs can serve as slides for projectors (Ill. 5). They are also ideal for mapmaking.

1

2

3

4

5

crayon

nature of the medium

crayons

Of the many art materials, probably none is more familiar than wax crayons. The fact that most of us were introduced to them at a tender age may influence us to think that they are beneath the dignity of more mature artists. Such is not the case: examples abound of distinguished drawings executed in this humble medium, although few can be dated before the nineteenth century.

Crayons consist of an oily or waxy binder impregnated with pigments. Records exist of a variety of prescriptions for binders, involving soap, salad oil, linseed oil, spermaceti, and beeswax. Crayons are of various types, some soft, some semihard; some are specifically designed for lithographic work, others for general classroom use.

Crayons work well on most papers. They do not blend well; when attempts are made to do this, the wax often "tears." Thus, most drawings are linear in character. Crayons can be scraped thin to produce semitransparent layers of subtle color, and they can be coated with black and scratched through, for crayon etchings.

This is an ideal medium for children; it is bold, colorful, clean, and inexpensive.

crayon etching

procedure

1. Cover the entire surface of the paper with a heavy coat of brightly colored crayons in either a free or a planned design. Avoid using dark colors. The heavier the colors are applied the better the final result. No definite drawing or design is necessary at this point.
2. Crayon over the brightly colored crayoned surface with black, violet, or any dark color, until no original color shows. Rubbing the crayon-covered surface with a piece of tissue or cloth first will help the dark crayon adhere.
3. Having a definite design or drawing in mind, scratch or scrape through the dark surface to the color or colors beneath.

supplies

1. Wax crayons
2. Drawing paper (white or manila)
3. Scraping tool (scissors, stick, hairpin, comb, nail, nail file, etc.)

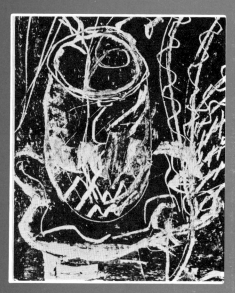

crayon doodle designs

supplies

1. Paper
2. Pencil
3. Crayons or paint

procedure

1. Cover the entire area of the paper with a continuous line drawn with complete spontaneity in light pencil. Make sure this line contains numerous directions made by a variety of straight and curved lines.
2. Look for shapes that are created by the lines and draw them in with a heavy pencil line. Many interesting abstract designs, as well as subject matter, can be found.
3. Crayon or paint the finished picture.

Note: The top doodle was the beginning of each drawing below it. Colored circles indicate the starting points of the doodles.

Original Doodle

Horizontal Design from Doodle

Vertical Design from Same Doodle

Original Doodle

Design from Doodle

74   crayon

crayon on cloth

procedure

1. Draw directly on the cloth with the crayons, using considerable pressure.
2. Melt the crayon into the cloth by placing it under a heat lamp or ironing over it between sheets of paper.

Note: The color will be semi-permanent only if the fabric is washed in *cool* water with a *nondetergent* soap.

supplies

1. Wax crayons
2. Heat lamp or hot iron
3. Cotton fabric, which must be washed thoroughly to cleanse it of all sizing or stiffener

crayon over tempera paint

supplies

1. Tempera paints and brush
2. Wax crayons
3. Paper
4. Sponge

procedure

1. Create the desired painting with tempera paints.
2. Work a contrasting color over each area with crayon, using moderate pressure.
3. Immerse the sponge in water; then "wash" the painting until the underlying tempera paint begins flaking off. The result will be a mottled, textured quality in which the residual crayon will supplement and accent the varied tempera tones that remain. The degree of flaking may be accelerated by brushing or, if it has gone too far, retouching may be done with the crayon.

Note: This procedure may be modified by applying the crayons more heavily, then holding the drawing under water that is just hot enough to melt them. The use of hot water necessitates a degree of caution.

crayon resist

procedure

1. Color drawing or design heavily with crayons, allowing areas of paper to show.
2. Cover the entire surface of the paper with watercolor paint. The paint will be absorbed by the uncolored paper and resisted by the wax crayons.

Note: If light-colored or white crayons are used, a dark watercolor wash will be most satisfactory.

supplies

1. Wax crayon
2. Paper
3. Brush
4. Watercolor paints
5. Water container

supplies

1. Crayons
2. Manila paper
3. Pencil
4. Watercolors
5. Brush

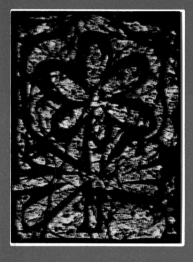

crayon resist batik

procedure

1. Make a light drawing in pencil on manila or heavy wrapping paper.
2. Using the pencil lines as a guide, draw lines and shapes with the crayon, allowing areas of the paper to show through.
3. Soak paper in water and crumple into a ball.
4. Uncrumple the paper, flatten and blot off excess water.
5. Paint the entire surface with watercolor paint or diluted tempera paint. The paint will be absorbed by the uncolored paper and resisted by the wax crayon, creating a weblike or batik pattern.

crayon rubbing

procedure

1. Making an outline drawing or design with pencil on thin drawing paper.
2. Hold the drawing against a surface that has a definite texture and rub the crayon over all areas of the drawing in which the texture will create a pleasing pattern. The texture will be transferred to the paper by the crayon.
3. Place the paper against another texture and transfer this texture to another portion of the drawing.
4. Textures may be repeated or overlapped.
5. Unusual effects can be obtained by using several colors.

supplies

1. Wax crayon
2. Thin drawing paper
3. Pencil
4. Textured surface

crayon shavings

supplies

1. Old electric iron
2. Wax crayons
3. Paper
4. Knife
5. Cardboard

procedure

1. Make a simple rack to hold the electric iron with the ironing surface up.
2. Shave the wax crayons with a knife, catching the shavings on a piece of paper fastened to cardboard. Push the shavings around until the image is created.
3. Pass the paper above the heated iron until the crayon shavings begin to melt. Continue this process with additional crayon until the desired pattern is created.
4. Watercolor, crayons, or tempera paint can be used to add detail to complete the picture.

Note: Care should be taken in this activity while handling the iron and knife. Heat sources other than the iron may be used to melt the shavings. The drawing may be laid in direct sunlight, on a radiator, or over a light bulb. Care should be taken in that too much exposure will make the wax run.

80   crayon

crayon textures

procedure

1. Hold the drawing paper against a surface that has a definite texture and rub the crayon over the paper. The texture will be transferred to the paper by the crayon.
2. Place the paper against another texture and transfer this texture to the paper.
3. Textures may be repeated or overlapped.

supplies

1. Wax crayon
2. Thin drawing paper
3. Pencil
4. Textured surface

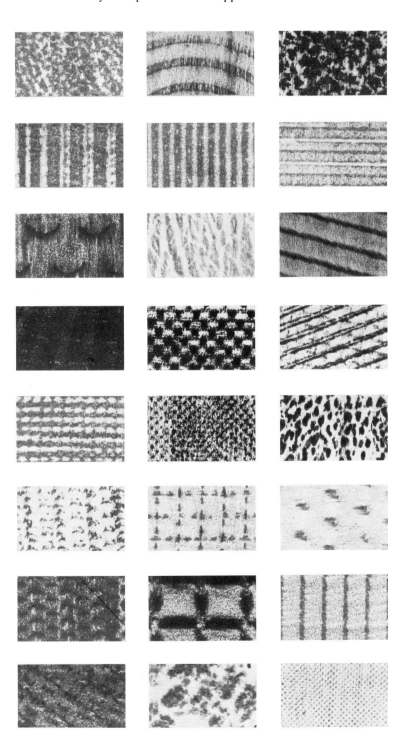

crayon transfer print

procedure

1. Completely cover a sheet of white paper with a heavy coating of light-colored chalk.
2. Cover the coating of chalk with a very heavy layer of darker colored crayon.
3. Place a piece of white paper containing a drawing (Ill. 1) over the crayon and chalk-covered paper.
4. Using a dull pencil or ball-point pen, and using pressure, trace over the drawing (Ill. 2).
5. The pressure causes the crayon to adhere to the underside of the drawing (Ill. 3) and creates a separate drawing on the crayon and chalk covered paper (Ill. 4).

1

2

3

4

encaustic painting

Encaustic is an old method of painting and pertains to the use of heated wax, which contains colored pigment. However, encaustic painting is also possible without a hot plate by soaking fine crayon shavings in a small amount of turpentine for twelve to fifteen days. The finer the shaving, the quicker it dissolves. The dissolved crayons should be a smooth, creamy medium for painting.

procedure

1. Sort out the pieces of crayon in a muffin tin according to color.
2. To melt the crayons, heat the muffin tin with an electric hot plate or light bulb.
3. Paint directly on the chosen surface with the hot melted crayons. Many varied effects of luminosity, texture, and tone are unique to encaustic painting.

Note: The addition of toluene (which should be obtainable through a chemistry department) in a volume equal to that of the melted crayon will facilitate the painting process by keeping the crayon in a liquid state. Toluene is extremely volatile and should be handled with caution.

supplies

1. Wax crayons, or see formula for encaustic paint, page 248.
2. Old muffin tin
3. A 100 or 150 watt light bulb and extension cord, or small electric hot plate or double boiler (to be used in melting crayons)
4. Stiff bristle painting brushes (the use of melted crayon will render the brushes unusable for any other media)
5. Any durable painting surface (wood, canvas board, plaster, masonite, heavy cardboard, etc.)
6. Turpentine and soap for cleaning brush

supplies

1. Road map
2. Tracing paper (translucent)
3. Pencil
4. Crayons or paint

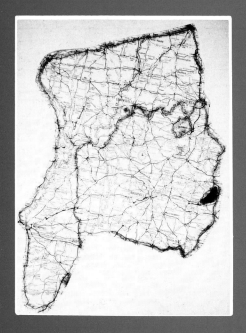

map doodle

procedure

1. Cover an area of the road map with a piece of tracing paper.
2. Look for shapes that are created by the roads on the map and draw them in with pencil. Many interesting abstract designs or subject matter can be found.
3. Crayon or paint the finished picture.

melted crayon

procedure

1. Hold the crayon briefly over the flame of the candle until it softens, then press, drip, or drag the softened crayon onto the paper. A definite design or drawing can be sketched on the paper beforehand to serve as a guide or the idea can be created with melted crayon directly.
2. Should the crayon become too short to hold over the flame, a long pin stuck into the crayon will solve this problem.
3. A number of different colors melted on top of one another will not only create an unusual textural effect, but will greatly enrich the color.

Note: As this problem involves the use of an open flame, it is suggested that every precaution be observed. White and yellow crayons can be heated, but should not be held in the flame for long as they will carbon.

supplies

1. Paper
2. Crayons with paper wrapping removed
3. Candle

pressed crayon laminations

supplies

1. Crayons
2. Wax paper
3. Iron
4. Knife or crayon sharpener
5. Newsprint or newspaper

procedure

1. Shave the crayons on a piece of wax paper placed on newspaper, creating the image by pushing the shavings around with a small piece of cardboard.
2. Cover the crayon-covered wax paper with another piece of wax paper.
3. Cover both pieces of wax paper with a piece of newspaper and iron with a warm iron.

Note: Variations are possible by cutting the wax laminations into various shapes and putting them into a design pressed again between two new sheets of wax paper. A string pressed between the wax sheets makes it adaptable for use in a mobile.

lettering

principles of lettering

Lettering and manuscript writing is an art that must conform to certain principles in order to be attractive and legible. There is no better time to learn these principles than in the formative years. There are, of course, many types of lettering and these are capable of many types of expression (i.e.—speed, action, dignity, beauty, etc.). However, the beginner should not venture too far from the simpler forms of lettering; and for this reason, only the fundamental rules of the Gothic letter structure are illustrated here. A variety of lettering can be created from this basic type, as is indicated in the accompanying illustration.

Lettering is one of those rare areas in the field of art where definite rules seem justified. To help produce better learning and manuscript writing in the grades, a few simple guides are listed. Each of these guidelines is subject to variation in more complicated styles, such as italic (slanted) or script.

It is recommended that a rough layout of the letters be done in pencil before inking.

Full consideration should be given to forms of the letters, size, placement of words on page, and spacing between letters and words.

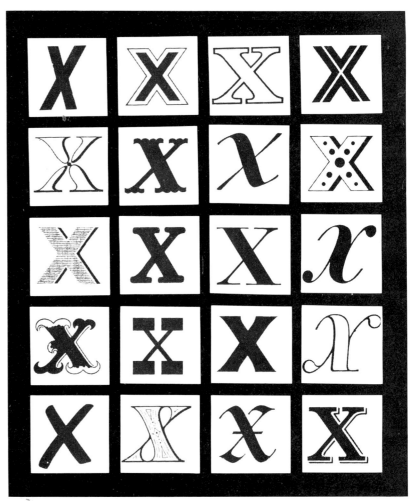

A basic letter with numerous variations.

ink or felt pen lettering

procedure

1. The axes of all Gothic letters are perpendicular to the line upon which they rest and are of uniform thickness.

PERPENDICULAR | perpendicular

2. Capitals or uppercase letters are all the same height—usually two spaces high for children.

ABCDEFGHIJKLMN
OPQRSTUVWXYZ·
1 2 3 4 5 6 7 8 9 0

3. Capital letters are of three different width groups—wide, average, and narrow.

Narrow Letters   Wide Letters

EFIJLT   GMOQW

There are no serifs or dots on the basic Gothic letters I or J, as indicated above, unless used on all letters.

4. A serif is a cross stroke on the end of the individual lines of a letter.

COLOR ART CRAFT

5. Horizontal line intersections generally should be above or below the middle of the letter for greater legibility.

Letters with horizontal   Letters with horizontal
line intersection above   line intersections below
the middle: the middle:

BEFHX   AGKPRY

supplies

1. Ink
2. Lettering pen and pen holder, or felt pen
3. Paper
4. Ruler
5. Pencil

6. Correct spacing is absolutely necessary to make lettering or manuscript writing legible and attractive. Measured spacing produces a lack of unity in lettered words. Spacing should be done with feeling for the *area between* the letters. Leave the width of an average letter between words when lettering.

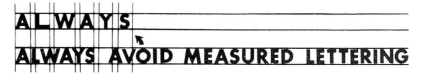

7. Lowercase, or small letters, are usually divided into thirds for the convenience of young children.

abcdefghijklmnop

qrstuvwxyz

8. The lowercase Gothic alphabet can be divided into three families of letters:

Short letters

aceimnorsuvwxz

Letters with ascenders

bdfhklt

(note that the letter t extends only halfway into the top space)

Letters with descenders

cut paper letters

procedure

1. Cut a number of strips of paper measured to the height of the proposed letters (Ill. 1).
2. Although all of the letters are of the same height, they are divided into three widths: wide, average, and narrow. The wide letter is a square and is made by folding the bottom corner up against the top of the strip, and cutting along the edge of the triangle thus formed (Ill. 2). Cut a considerable number of these shapes (Ill. 3).
3. The average width letter is made by cutting away a portion of the square (Ill. 4). Cut a number of these of the same width.
4. The narrow letter is made by cutting another portion from the average width letter. Cut a number of these of the same width (Ill.5).
5. A supply of shapes for each size letter has now been provided. The paper size must be selected according to the width of the letter chosen and can be cut according to the instructions that follow.

supplies

1. Lightweight paper (typing paper works well)
2. Scissors
3. Pencil
4. Ruler
5. Paste or rubber cement

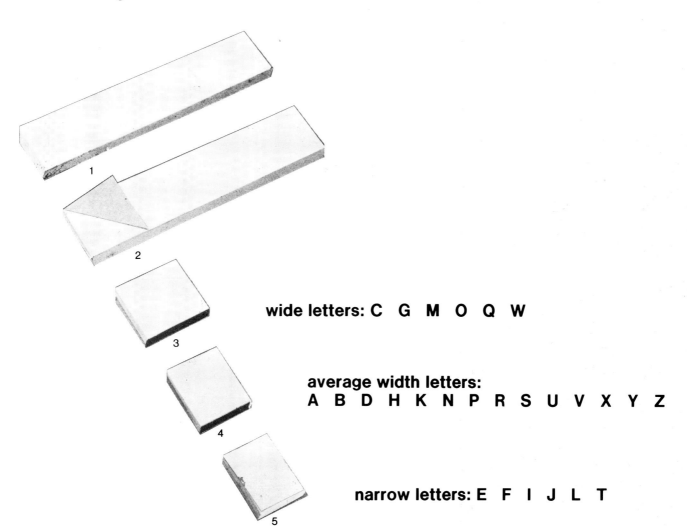

wide letters: C G M O Q W

average width letters:
A B D H K N P R S U V X Y Z

narrow letters: E F I J L T

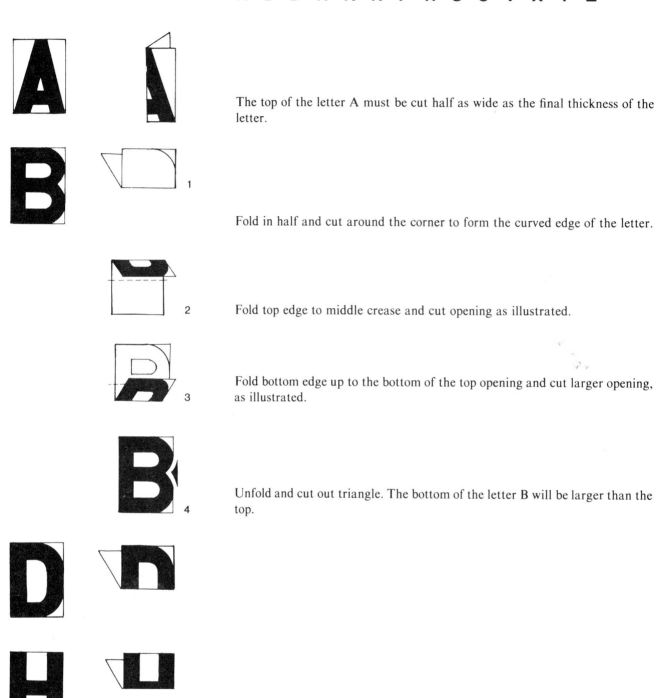

The top of the letter A must be cut half as wide as the final thickness of the letter.

1

Fold in half and cut around the corner to form the curved edge of the letter.

2

Fold top edge to middle crease and cut opening as illustrated.

3

Fold bottom edge up to the bottom of the top opening and cut larger opening, as illustrated.

4

Unfold and cut out triangle. The bottom of the letter B will be larger than the top.

The crossbar of the letter H must be cut half as wide as the final thickness of the letter.

This letter K is cut without folding the paper.

The N cannot be folded to cut.

Fold top edge down below the middle and cut out shape as illustrated.

The opening in the letter R is cut like the P; the remainder of the letter is cut without folding.

Fold paper in half, then in half again. Cut a rounded corner.

Open and cut away the areas marked with X.

Open and cut away the excess paper from the figure 8 to form the letter S.

The bottom of the letter V must be cut half as wide as the final thickness of the letter.

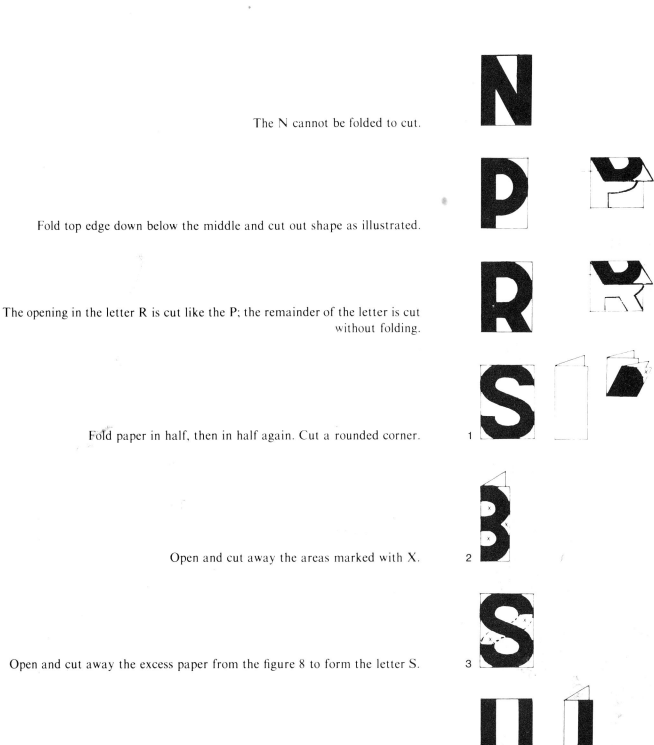

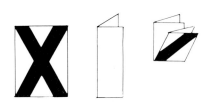

The center of the letter X must be cut half as wide as the final thickness of the letter.

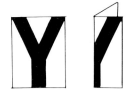

The stem of the letter Y must be cut half as wide as the final thickness of the letter.

The Z cannot be folded to cut.

narrow letters: E F I J L T

Shorten the middle arm of the E. The middle arm of the letter E must be cut half as wide as the final thickness of the letter.

For the F, shorten the middle arm and remove bottom leg. The middle arm of the letter F must be cut half as wide as the final thickness of the letter.

The letter J is a narrow letter, but is cut like the letter U.

The L cannot be folded to cut.

The stem of the letter T must be cut half as wide as the final thickness of the letter.

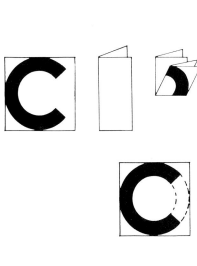

Fold paper in half, then in half again. Cut quarter circle for both outside and inside of letter.

Open and cut away the section indicated.

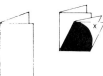

Fold paper in half, then in half again. Cut quarter circle for outside of letter only.

Unfold and cut out openings in the areas indicated.

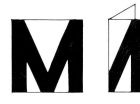

Open and cut away the parts indicated.

The middle bottom of the letter M must be cut half as wide as the final thickness of the letter. The sides of the M are vertical. The middle of the M should go to the bottom.

Fold paper in half, then in half again. Cut quarter circle for both outside and inside of letter.

Fold paper in half, then in half again. Cut as indicated.

Open and cut away the extra tails—or cut like the letter O and add a separate piece for the tail.

The middle top of the letter W must be cut half as wide as the final thickness of the letter. The sides of the W slant. The middle of the W should go to the top.

The top or bottom of the following letters can either be pointed or flat, but all must be of the same style when used together in forming a word. Pointed letters should extend either above or below the line.

AA VV NN ZZ
WW MM

Simple three-dimensional lettering is interesting to use and easy to make.

Fold a sheet of paper so that it is twice the height of the intended letter. Fold the paper in half again if the letter can be folded to cut. Make sure when cutting that each letter is held together by some part of the fold.

Mount the bottom of the letters on a poster or bulletin board— the spring in the paper will give the top half a three-dimensional effect.

paper strip letters

procedure

1. Cut paper strips of uniform width.
2. Form the letters as illustrated, adjusting the paper to the desired size. Cut off the excess portion of the strip, if any.
3. Glue the parts of the letters as necessary.
4. Apply glue to the bottom edge of each letter in turn, and fix in place to form desired words.

supplies

1. Paper
2. Scissors
3. Paste or glue

matting and framing

mat proportions

The matting of display material is an additional cost, but it makes displays more effective and is a practical method of retaining and storing outstanding material. It should be pointed out that display material of similar size is interchangeable, enabling the mat to be used more than once.

For effective and proper matting of creative art work and other display material, the following rules generally apply:

The optical center of a picture area is always a certain distance above the measured center. Measured centering of a work in a mat therefore creates a top heavy appearance, whereas optical centering creates greater frontality and balance, and more comfortable viewing.

1. In matting a square illustration the top and sides of the mat should be equal, with the bottom margin wider (Ill. 1).
2. In matting a vertical rectangular illustration the bottom margin is the widest, and the top margin wider than the sides (Ill. 2).
3. In matting a horizontal rectangular illustration, the bottom margin is the widest and the top margin should be smaller than the sides (Ill. 3).

1

2

3

cutting a mat

procedure

1. Cut the mat board large enough to accommodate the picture to be matted, including a generous margin (Ill. 1).
2. Cut a piece of cardboard of equal dimensions. This piece will be the backing for the finished mat (Ill. 2).
3. Using the suggestions for square, horizontal, or vertical pictures mentioned earlier, measure and draw a light line the size of the opening to be cut on the face of the mat board (Ill. 3). Be sure that these lines are drawn at least one-half of an inch smaller than both the length and width of the actual picture to be mounted. This will allow the mat to overlap the picture on all sides.

supplies

1. Mat board (pebbled or smooth, colored or white)
2. Cardboard (which should be of the same rigidity as the mat board)
3. Pencil
4. Ruler
5. Mat knife or single-edge razor blade
6. Gummed tape

1

2

3

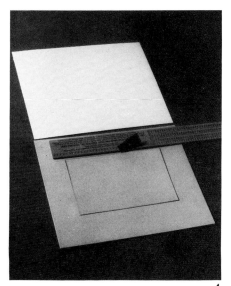

4

5

6

7

8

9

4. Place a piece of heavy scrap cardboard under the line to be cut. Cut carefully along the pencil lines with a sharp mat knife or single-edge razor blade. Apply enough pressure on the tool to cut through the mat with one cut if possible. A ruler held firmly will serve as a guide while cutting. If the cutting tool is held at a forty-five degree angle, a beveled edge can be cut—but only after considerable practice (Ill. 4).

5. Turn the mat over and butt the top edge of the second piece of cardboard. Hinge the two pieces together with gummed tape (Ill. 5).

6. Close the mat on the cardboard with the window opening facing up. Mark the four corners of the opening on the cardboard backing with a sharp pencil. This will help in locating the picture directly behind the window (Ill. 6).

7. Open the mat again and center the picture behind the window, making sure that the closed mat overlaps the picture on all four sides (Ill. 7).

8. Fasten the picture to the cardboard along the top edge with gummed tape (Ill. 8), making sure that the tape does not overlap the work far enough to be seen when the mat is closed. A picture fastened this way is easily removed and replaced with another without harm to the mat.

9. Finished matted picture (Ill. 9).

covered mat

procedure

1. Cut the mat as instructed on pages 103 and 104 (Ill. 1).
2. Select a piece of material which is larger than the mat (Ill. 2).
3. Cut the materials so it exceeds the measurements of the mat by about one inch or less (Ill. 3).
4. Cut the corners of the material diagonally up to the corners of the mat (Ill. 3).
5. With the mat still face down on the material, cut the inside corners of the material diagonally from the corners of the mat (Ill. 3). Leave about one-half inch of material around the window.
6. Place glue along inside and outside edges of the mat and fold back the material on these sides, gluing it down along the back (Ill. 4).

Note: Decorative trim, cord, or strips of paper may be added to the front of the mat around the window as desired to make it more decorative (Ill. 5).

supplies

1. Mat board or corrugated cardboard (see page 103)
2. Pencil
3. Ruler
4. Mat knife or heavy scissors
5. White glue
6. Cloth, wrapping paper, wallpaper, Contact paper

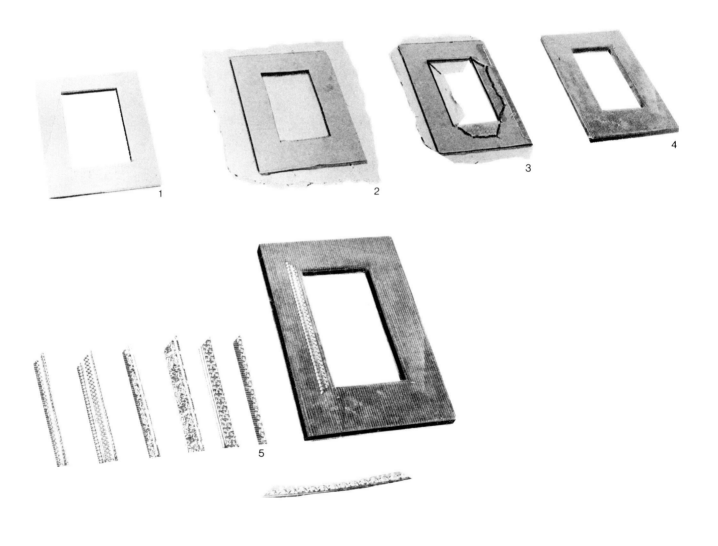

mounted picture mat

supplies

1. Picture to be matted
2. Mat board or colored cardboard
3. Rubber cement
4. Scissors, sharp knife, or single-edge razor blade
5. Pencil
6. Ruler

procedure

1. Choose picture to be mounted and cut it to the desired size.
2. Cut material to be used as mat large enough to accommodate the picture to be mounted, including a generous margin. Use matting proportions for square, horizontal, or vertical pictures on page 102 as a guide.
3. Place the cut picture on the mounting material and use a ruler to make sure the border proportions are correct.
4. Draw around the picture with a light pencil line.
5. Remove the picture and apply rubber cement to the pencil enclosed area. Allow to dry.
6. Apply rubber cement to the back of the picture and allow it to dry.
7. Carefully replace the picture in the penciled shape. Lay a clean piece of paper over the illustration and smooth it with the hand.

shadowbox frame

procedure

1. Select a box larger than the picture to be framed (Ill. 1).
2. Mount the picture or print (Ill. 2) to be framed on a piece of cardboard the size of the interior of the box. The cardboard left exposed will form a mat around the picture (Ill. 3).
3. Cut four cardboard strips with a forty-five degree angle at each end (Ill. 4). The shortest dimension of each strip should be slightly shorter than the box.
4. Glue these four strips at the corners to form a flat frame (Ill. 5).
5. Glue the decorative trim (Ill. 6) to the flat frame (Ill. 7).
6. Glue the mounted picture in the bottom of the box (Ill. 8).
7. Glue the decorative flat frame (Ill. 7) to the top edge of the box (Ill. 9).
8. Glue a picture hanger or cardboard support (Ill. 10) to the back of the box.

supplies

1. Shallow cardboard box, slightly larger than picture to be framed (Ill. 1)
2. Picture or print to be framed (Ill. 2)
3. White or colored cardboard for mounting picture (Ill. 3)
4. Colored cardboard for framing strips (Ill. 4)
5. Glue
6. Rubber cement for mounting picture
7. Decorative trim (Ill. 6)
8. Scissors or knife

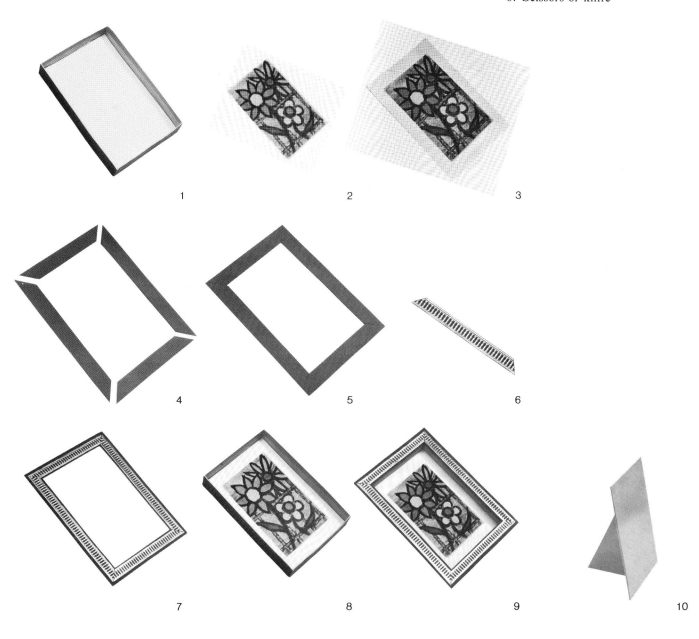

1
2
3

4
5
6

7
8
9
10

three-dimensional picture frame

supplies

1. Cardboard
2. Ruler
3. Scissors, single-edge razor blade, or knife
4. Pencil
5. Rubber cement

procedure

1. Choose the picture to be framed and mount with rubber cement on a piece of cardboard, allowing at least one and one half inches of cardboard on all sides (Ill. 1).
2. Score around the edge of the mounted picture deep enough so it can be bent forward (Ill. 1).
3. Cut out four V-shaped corners. The larger the V, the deeper the frame (Ill. 2).
4. Turn up all sides until corners meet.
5. Hold corners together and tape on back (Ill. 3).
6. To hang, place a piece of tape across two ends of a loop of string, fastening them toward the top of the back.

1

2

3

murals

murals

A mural is a large work of art usually designed for a specific location and intended to be viewed by large numbers of people.

A small mural may be produced by the individual while a larger work is readily adaptable as a group enterprise. As such, and because of its mass audience, it can be developed from a theme of general interest selected from any subject area.

As a public work of art, some consideration should be given to effective placement of the mural in terms of traffic, lighting, and other factors. When the location has been determined the space available will help to decide the total shape of the mural. Architecture may be a friend or foe; in any case, it must be considered.

Those participating in the design of a mural should be of a narrow age range. When older people are mixed with younger children, there is often an unfortunate tendency to compare. Actually, when ages vary, the products are noncomparable, but this is not always understood, and the general reaction could be frustrating and embarrassing to some.

When the main composition has been sketched, the surface (wrapping paper is cheap, strong, and quite adequate) may be divided up into a working area for each person. Because of spatial restrictions, it is not always possible to have all artists working simultaneously. Work could proceed on a shift basis, integrating this project with other scheduled activities.

It is usually advisable to restrict the work on a mural to one or two media. Materials are variable in strength, and the design could be chaotic if all media were used, unless they were subject to some type of coordination. Some media, such as chalk, are perfectly satisfactory but quite impermanent and could be easily smudged during the process of the work. In avoiding this, a fixative or plastic spray could be used to protect the drawing, but this would ruin the surface for further drawing. Crayon is cheap and permanent; poster paint is effective, but may flake off if the mural is rolled up or mistreated. Cut paper is a simple and effective medium and is easily combined with other media. Collage techniques may be employed by pasting up fabrics and other textured materials; and papier collé may be used according to the instructions under the problem "Magazine Collé."

mural techniques

Permanent painted wall mural.

procedure

1. Discuss murals past and present, as well as the selected theme.
2. Produce idea sketches.
3. Enlarge selected sketches on wrapping paper (Ill. 1, 2, and 3).
4. Cut out the large sketches like paper dolls.
5. Paint the wall with roller and latex paint (Ill. 4).
6. Stretch wrapping paper below the wall. Arrange the cut-out shapes on the wrapping paper, using a small loop of masking tape on the back.
7. Make changes by shifting the cut-outs on the wrapping paper as necessary.
8. When satisfied with arrangement, draw around cut-outs with pencil on the wall (Ill. 5), and return cut-outs to wrapping paper (Ill. 6).
9. Paint the wall design with latex paint, giving every child an opportunity to paint (Ill. 7).
10. Complete background and details with brush or sponge (see sponge painting, page 129) (Ill. 8).
11. Black and/or white paint may be used to outline or add detail.

Note: Have a group clean brushes and wipe up any spills.

supplies

1. Paper
2. Crayons
3. Wrapping paper
4. Scissors
5. Masking tape
6. Pencils
7. Latex paint (semigloss)
8. Brushes, large and small
9. Rollers
10. Sponges
11. Old shirts (for smocks)
12. Cans with lids, to hold various colored paints

2

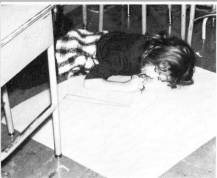

3

1

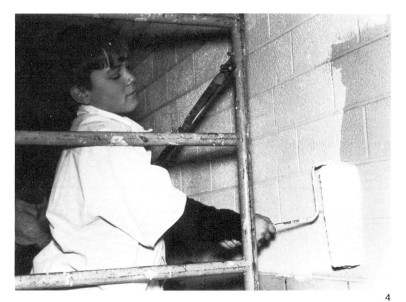

4

5

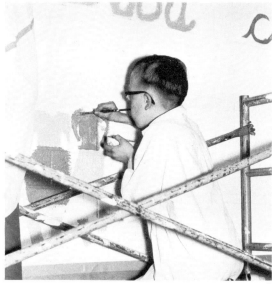

7

6

8

112   murals

chalk mural

procedure

1. Discuss murals past and present, as well as the selected theme.
2. Produce idea sketches.
3. Enlarge selected sketches on wrapping paper (Ill. 1, 2, and 3).
4. Draw with chalks on paper covered chalkboard or on chalkboard itself.

Note: A chalkboard mural is suitable only when the chalkboard surface can be spared for a period of time. If adequate chalkboard space is available, chalkboard murals make particularly effective holiday projects.

supplies

1. Colored chalks
2. Wrapping paper or chalkboard

crayon mural

procedure

1. Discuss murals past and present, as well as the selected theme.
2. Produce idea sketches.
3. Enlarge selected sketches on wrapping paper (Ill. 1, 2, and 3). Crayons are not suitable for use on walls or chalkboards.
4. Older children possessed of patience may like to do parts of the mural in the crayon etching technique (see page 73).

supplies

1. Crayons
2. Wrapping paper

cut paper mural

procedure

1. Discuss murals past and present, as well as the selected theme.
2. Produce idea sketches.
3. Enlarge selected sketches on wrapping paper (Ill. 1, 2, and 3).
4. Cut out the subjects and pin or paste them to the bulletin board or paper background.

supplies

1. Drawing paper
2. Painting or drawing materials for any technique chosen
3. Paper or bulletin board background
4. Pins, paste, or glue
5. Scissors

tempera mural

procedure

1. Discuss murals past and present as well as the selected theme.
2. Produce idea sketches.
3. Enlarge selected sketches on wrapping paper (Ill. 1, 2, and 3).
4. Paint the mural on the paper or on the chalkboard.

Note: A painted chalkboard mural is easily washed off because tempera paint is not a waterproof paint.

supplies

1. Tempera paints
2. Brushes
3. Wrapping paper or chalkboard

paint and ink

nature of the medium

watercolor

Watercolor is a brilliant, transparent, water-soluble painting medium. The pigment is available as color blocks in pans, or in the more expensive and professional tubes.

The distinguishing property of watercolor is the sparkling quality resulting from its transparency. Most painters strive for a spontaneous effect by utilizing the whiteness of the paper and the fluid blending of the colors. Watercolor requires planning, as does any art form, but there can be a good deal of improvisation. Unlike oil paintings, watercolors are worked up quickly, and rarely reworked.

The prerequisite to the successful use of watercolor is familiarity with its effects, achieved only through experimentation. Prior to painting the paper should be dampened; after this one should try bold, wet washes, with intermingled colors. Bold and fine strokes should be attempted, both wet and dry. One can also try wet-on-dry techniques, blotting, tilting the paper to control the flow of color, various resists, and combinations of watercolor with other media. For serious efforts, it is recommended that the paper be fastened to a board with paper tape after soaking, to allow the painting to dry without distortion of the paper.

Three types of paper are available for watercolor painting:

    Hot-pressed: a smooth paper, for detailed work
    Cold-pressed: moderate texture, and the most common
    Rough: highly-textured surface, producing clear, sharp effects

These are the more "professional" papers beyond the needs and means of most children. A paper of fairly heavy weight should be used, however; manila (or its equivalent) is a satisfactory, inexpensive paper.

Brushes used for watercolor painting should be washed frequently, and the cleaning water should be replaced often. Smocks or aprons are useful, as are newspapers and paper towels. Expect a mess; it's the only way to learn!

tempera paint

Tempera is a water-soluble paint that is available as liquid or dry powder. It is an extremely versatile medium and works well on a variety of surfaces. (When painted on nonporous materials, a small amount of liquid detergent should be added.)

Tempera may be spread by brush, roller, sponge, stick, or, if slightly reduced with water, it can be sprayed. Lights and darks are controlled by additions of white or black.

Unlike watercolor, tempera is an opaque medium; the appearance of the paper is not such a factor nor does it have to be stretched. The paint may be mixed semidry and built up to create a textured surface. The other possibilities are too great to list here, but include the following: screen printing, block-printing, finger painting, and lettering.

Young children using a potentially messy medium such as tempera should wear smocks, if possible. Clear water should be kept handy for keeping brushes clean. Small plastic or paper cups can be provided for the various colors.

inks

A liquid vehicle and a soluble pigment are required for making ink, and this is satisfactory only if it can flow evenly, and has good tinting strength. The earliest ink known, black carbon, was prepared by the early Egyptians and Chinese. This was followed by iron-gall (from growths on trees), bistre (burnt wood), and sepia (a secretion from cuttle fish). Today, there is a wide variety of inks, transparent and opaque, water-soluble and waterproof. Perhaps the type best known to the art student is India ink, which is really a waterproof carbon black. All of these inks serve effectively for *line* drawings; drawing *washes* are usually produced with ink sticks or water colors. A tremendous number of inks can be made with fruit and vegetable juices, aniline, and coal dyes.

Pen and ink drawings are generally characterized by their clarity and precision. This, of course, can be modified by choice of instrument or method of control. It takes a great many strokes to produce an area of tone, and this is the principal reason why pen and ink drawings are best created on a fairly small scale.

pens

Those of us who take our familiar metal pen points of various kinds for granted may not realize that they are fairly new, not having been successfully developed until the last century. Until that time, the reed pen had been the pen of the ancients, and the quill pen the principal instrument from the medieval period to modern times. Most of us probably remember the use of quill pens in the drawings of Rembrandt and in the historical documents drawn up by the founders of our Republic.

Today, the advent of ball, felt, and plastic tip pens have revolutionized the writing industry, as well as providing artists with yet another drawing tool. Artists, however, still make use of the earlier pen types on occasion, and even resort, at times, to match sticks and other unlikely things for making ink marks on paper. Each drawing instrument leaves its own distinctive mark and, for the artist, has its own special interests and disciplines. In the hands of children, the mechanical metal points and felt and plastic tips are generally more suitable, but other kinds of pens might provide some exciting moments for the older child.

brushes*

Bristle is obtained from the body of hogs and boars found in Russia, Japan, Formosa, Korea, France, Central and Eastern Europe. While all animal hair has "points," bristle has "flags" (the individual bristle splits into two or three tiny forks on the end). Only pure natural white and black bristle with their original flags preserved are used in Delta brushes.

Brown Squirrel Hair, known as Kazan, is generally found in the Kazan Region of Russia. It has finer points and is more elastic than other squirrel hair, making it ideal for camel hair water color brushes.

Camel Hair is the trade name for squirrel hair and pony hair. Squirrel hair is obtained from the tails of various types of Russian squirrels (Scuirus Vulgaris Calotus).

*Courtesy Delta Brush, Division of Binney and Smith, Inc.

Golden Nylon is a synthetic tapered filament especially suited for use with acrylic and polymer paints. Delta blends finely tapered nylon filaments of various diameters to assure the right amount of resiliency and a fine working edge.

Ox Hair—The best grades are selected and prepared from ox ear hair found in Central Europe and certain parts of North and South America. Ox ear hair with its strong body and fine tapered points is especially suited for brushes used in oil or heavier colors, since it will hold plenty of color, retain its elasticity, and perform smoothly. It will also perform well for show card and water color brushes, though here again the special qualities of red sable hair cannot be equaled.

Pony Hair is obtained from pony hides. It ranges in color from light to dark brown, is straight and soft but does not have the fine points that distinguish squirrel hair.

Red Sable Hair —The most valuable hair used in artist brushes is obtained from the tail of the kolinsky (Mustela Sibirica) found in the Amur Region of Siberia, and in The Republic of Korea. Red sable hair, pale red in color with darker tips, has special qualities unmatched by any other hair—strength along with slim body, extremely fine points, and great resiliency. Not only will it come to a needle-fine point or knife-like edge, but will retain its full elasticity, making it virtually irreplaceable for the best brushes used in any water color medium.

Sabeline Hair is specially treated silken ox hair, light in color with exceptional points, and lots of snap. Delta applies the trade name "Golden Sable" to a selected sabeline hair, whose properties most closely resemble those of red sable hair.

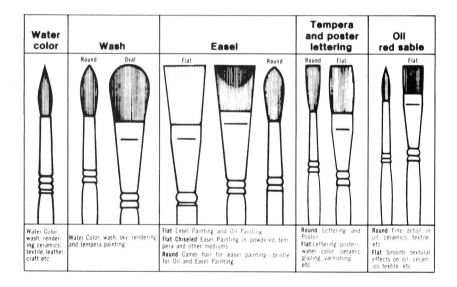

the care and use of brushes

1. Use watercolor brushes for watercolor and oil brushes for oil. Do not mix.
2. Clean brushes after each use. Neglect will cause the brush to lose its shape.
3. Never rest a brush vertically on its hairs. Suspend it, if possible; if not, rest it on its side.

cleaning procedures

1. Water-based brush media

   a. Repeatedly wash in cold water.
   b. Straighten the hairs to their natural shape before drying.
   c. Rinse repeatedly in clean water while in use.

2. Oil-based brush media

   a. Squeeze paint from the brush with waste paper or rags.
   b. Lather on the palm of the hand with soap and water.
   c. Rinse repeatedly until all paint is removed.
   d. Restore the original shape of the bristles.

3. Acrylic and polymer brush media

   a. Clean in cold water immediately after use.
   b. Clean in warm water if the paint has hardened.

Notes: Clean house paint, oil stain, enamel, or varnish with turpentine, proprietary brush cleaner or paint thinner.
Clean shellac or alcohol stain with alcohol.
For lacquer, use lacquer thinner.
Detergent soaps are effective for cleaning oil, acrylic, and watercolor brushes.

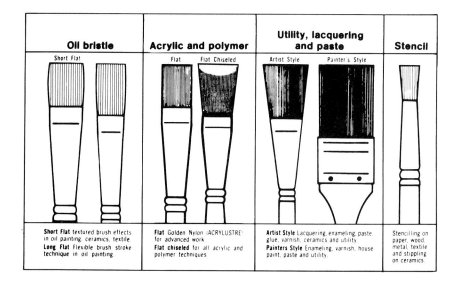

blottos

procedure

1. Cut a number of paper squares and rectangles of various sizes.
2. Crease each paper square in the middle so that later it can be folded easily.
3. Sprinkle a few drops of paint on one side of the crease.
4. Fold the paper on the creased line with the paint inside and press—this causes the paint to be squeezed into various and interesting shapes.
5. When the paper is opened the result will be surprising—it might resemble an insect, flower, butterfly, or any number of items.
6. After a number of blottos are made, cut them out and arrange them into a picture or pattern. When satisfied with the arrangement, paste them in place on a piece of paper of desired size.

Notes: After experimenting it will be possible to control the results by placing the paint according to a predetermined pattern.

Don't overlook the possibility of using several colors in one blotto or the adding of details with other media.

drawing with ink

procedure

1. Pen and ink drawing is capable of great interest if approached in an experimental manner. For instance, pen points of different types create varied lines and these lines in turn may be combined with each other to create stippled, cross-hatched, scumbled, and other textural effects.

2. Brush and ink drawing is a highly expressive medium due to the flexibility of the brush line. The quality of line may be controlled by the type of brush (bristle or sable), wide or narrow, fully or sparsely haired; the hand pressure applied; the quantity of ink carried by the brush; and the calculating or spontaneous attitude of the artist.

   As in most drawing, greater freedom is obtained from the brush by avoiding the grip used in writing. Instead, one may hold the brush between the thumb and forefingers while supporting the hand on the other three fingers. The movement of the brush should be initiated with the body ("body english") and directed through the arm. Drawing done with the fingers or wrists is more suited to the development of surface details.

3. Stick and ink is a lesser known drawing procedure, but one that has enough individuality to justify its frequent use. In technique it is very simple—one merely dips an absorbent piece of wood into the ink, allows it to become semi-saturated and draws as one would with a pen. Interesting effects may be obtained by using sticks with frayed, sharp, broad, and smooth ends.

Note: Ink is very effective when used with other media. It may be added to watercolor, tempera, and crayon to enhance the brilliance of colors or provide accents and outline. The above may, in turn, be used over ink. When ink is used on wet paper, the results are unexpected and interesting.

supplies

1. Pen
2. Brush
3. Soft wood sticks of various types (match sticks, popsicle sticks, etc.)
4. Ink
5. Paper

supplies

1. Paper, paper-covered object, or cloth
2. Multicolored felt tip pens
3. Pencil
4. Clear spray

felt tip pen drawing

procedure

1. Until confidence is gained, use preliminary light outline drawing in pencil on paper.
2. Areas of the drawing can now be filled in with colored felt tip pens.
3. To prevent possible smudging, spray with clear spray.

Note: Part of the fun of drawing with felt tip pens is experimenting for new effect.

finger painting

procedure

1. Soak the paper in water in any of the following ways, making sure both sides are thoroughly wet.

   A. Put the paper under the faucet in a sink, or
   B. Roll the paper into a tube and submerge it in a container of water, or
   C. Spread the paper on a table and soak it with sponge and water. The paper adheres more firmly to a surface if wet on both sides.

2. Place the wet paper on a smooth and flat surface. Do not place it too close to the edge of the table top, as the paint may drip over. Make sure the glossy side of the paper is up and all wrinkles and air bubbles are smoothed out. Satisfactory finger paintings cannot be made on an uneven or unsteady surface.
3. Place approximately one tablespoonful of finger paint on the wet paper— if powdered finger paint is used, sift it lightly over the entire paper—more can be applied later if necessary. Paint applied too heavily will crack or chip off when dry.
4. Spread the paint evenly over the entire surface of paper with the palm of the hand or forearm to create the background of the finger painting.
5. Varied movements of the hands and forearms in various positions will create interesting effects. The side of the hand when held rigid and pulled over paper makes long and delicate leaves. This same hand position moved in a zig-zag motion creates an altogether different effect. Experiment with a variety of hand and arm movements and positions. An infinite number of effects are possible by using the closed fist, bent fingers, open palm, heel of the hand, wrist, etc. Other various effects can also be obtained by using a comb, a small notched piece of cardboard, etc. Areas of color can also be cleaned away with a sponge.
6. New beginnings can be made until the paper loses its gloss. Sprinkle a few drops of water on the paper if the finger paint becomes too sticky to allow the hand or arm to slide easily over the paper.
7. Spread the paper or newspaper on the floor in a seldom used area. Lift the finger painting by two corners and lay it on some newspapers.
8. Allow the painting to dry. Press it on the unpainted side with a hot iron.

Notes: It is suggested that only a few children work at one time unless a large room with adequate table space is available. Finger paintings can be used to decorate items of many kinds, including knitting boxes, wastebaskets, book jackets, portfolio covers, etc.

Colored paper cut to particular shapes and pasted in place on finger paintings adds further detail.

A stencil cut from paper and pasted over a finger painting is another variation. If finger painting is used as a decorative covering it should be sprayed with clear plastic spray or painted with shellac for permanence.

A comb or piece of notched paper will give good results if drawn through the wet paint.

supplies

1. Finger paint (recipe on page 249)
2. Glossy or glazed paper
3. Sponge
4. Iron
5. Plastic spray or white shellac
6. Water must be available in a sink or large container, to soak the paper

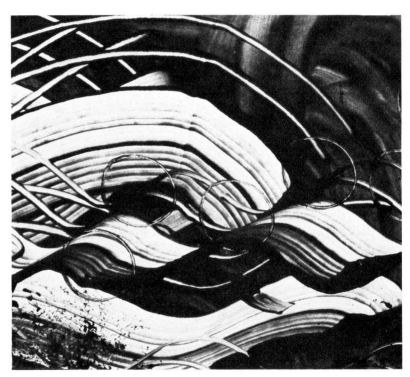

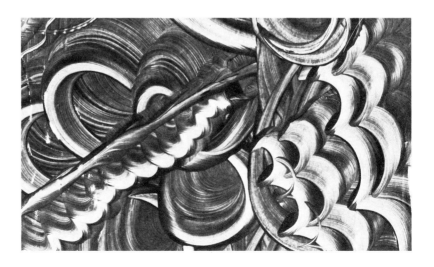

finger painting over crayon

procedure

1. Cover the paper with brightly colored crayon.
2. Lay the crayoned paper on a smooth flat surface.
3. Spread liquid starch over the crayon.
4. Sprinkle a small amount of tempera paint in liquid starch. Be sure that its color contrasts with the crayon color(s).
5. The color will mix as soon as the hand is drawn over the surface.

Note: See page 123 for finger painting instructions.

supplies

1. Drawing paper
2. Liquid starch
3. Powdered tempera
4. Crayons

supplies

1. Colored waterproof drawing ink
2. Cloth—unbleached muslin, silk, rayon, etc.
3. Brush, lettering pen, or felt pen
4. White blotting paper
5. Smooth flat board

ink or felt pen on cloth

procedure

1. Make a drawing or design with the pencil directly on the blotting paper.
2. Place the fabric directly over the drawing.
3. Painting with ink can begin when the drawing can be seen through the cloth due to its transparency. The blotter on which the pencil drawing was made creates an absorbent surface which will take up any excess paint.

Note: Do not use too much ink on the brush, but paint in a "dry brush" technique. Large areas should be built up with textures, such as dots, cross-hatching, series of dashes, etc.

pulled string design

procedure

1. Place a sheet of paper on a flat surface.
2. Coat the string thoroughly with paint or ink. If tempera paint is used, be sure it is thin.
3. Arrange the paint soaked string on the paper. Twisted loops in the string will make interesting effects. Allow one or two ends to extend beyond the same edge of the paper.
4. Place another piece of paper over this string arrangement.
5. Cover this paper with a firm piece of cardboard, wood, masonite, or magazine, and hold it in place lightly with one hand. With the other hand, grasp the ends of the string and pull it gently from between the papers.
6. Carefully peel the two papers apart. The design will be duplicated on the second sheet of paper.

supplies

1. String
2. Paper
3. Paint or ink
4. Board, heavy cardboard, masonite, magazine
5. Brush or sponge

supplies

1. Paper
2. Watercolor paint or thin tempera
3. Soda straws
4. Brush

procedure

1. Place several little pools of variously colored paint on the paper with a brush.
2. Point the end of the straw at the pools of paint and blow in the direction the paint is meant to move.
3. Overlapping of colors creates numerous effects in blending colors.
4. Add details when dry.

sponge painting

procedure

1. Soak the paper thoroughly in water.
2. Lay the wet paper on a smooth surface and remove all the wrinkles and excess water.
3. Use pieces of moist sponge which have been cut into small shapes and use as a brush by dipping them into the tempera paint.
4. Apply to moist paper that may have general areas of a design marked with a pencil.
5. Details and accents can be added with a brush when painting is dry.

Note: Experiment by trying this on both wet and dry paper. Also allow the color to mix and blend.

supplies

1. Sponge or cellulose sponge cut into a variety of sizes and shapes
2. Scissors
3. Watercolor or liquid tempera paint
4. Paper
5. Brush

tempera painting on damp paper

supplies

1. Dry or liquid tempera paint
2. Brush
3. Paper
4. Water container
5. Blotting material (rag, sponge, paper towel, etc.)

procedure

1. Soak the paper thoroughly in water.
2. Lay the wet paper on a desk top or drawing board and smooth out all the wrinkles.
3. Blot up any pools of water with blotting material.
4. Paint directly on the damp paper. Make sure to use more pigment than water, for the colors tend to lose their brilliance when dry. Paint light colors first, and second and third colors before the paper dries, so colors will mingle and blend into spontaneous and soft shapes. After the paint is applied, avoid reworking.
5. Leave some areas unpainted to add sparkle.
6. Details, if necessary, can be painted in when the painting is dry.

Note: Damp paper tempera painting must be done hurriedly to be lively. Don't expect complete success on the first try, for only experience will tell just how wet the paper must be and how much paint should be used. Clean the brush and the water in the container often.

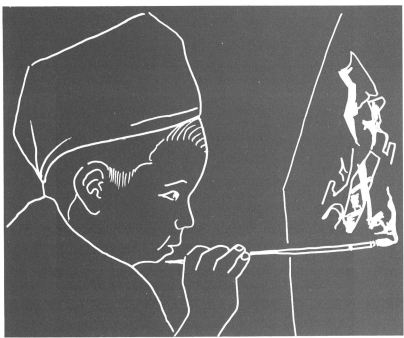

tempera resist

procedure

1. Paint some areas of the paper with tempera as necessary to suggest the design. By all means, leave much of the paper unpainted, thus making provision for the absorption of the ink by these areas. The paint used should be fairly heavy body.
2. When the paint is completely dry, paint over everything—tempera and paper—with India ink.
3. When the ink is dry, hold the drawing under running water, allowing the force of the water to dislodge the ink. Should this ink prove stubborn, its removal may be speeded by light strokes of the finger. A certain amount of caution should be exercised in removing the ink. Excessive washing could remove too much of the paint and ink. However, many seeming disasters have turned out beautifully at second glance. Furthermore, any lost color can be replaced with watercolor, ink, crayon, or tempera.

Note: If the color is to remain, it must be painted on the paper, not over another color.

supplies

1. Tempera paints
2. Brush
3. Paper
4. Higgins India ink

supplies

1. Watercolor paint
2. Paper
3. Rubber cement
4. Brush
5. Eraser

procedure

1. Paint a picture on the paper with rubber cement. Use the brush attached to the rubber cement jar or apply with a finger.
2. Allow the rubber cement to dry.
3. Paint over the rubber cement picture with watercolor paint. Several colors can be mingled together. The rubber cement will resist the paint.
4. Allow the paint to dry.
5. Clean away the rubber cement with an eraser and expose the paper and original drawing.

Note: Rubber cement can be painted over the areas previously painted with watercolor and repeated as often as desired. Make sure each is dry before applying the other.

watercolor painting on damp paper

procedure

1. Soak the paper thoroughly in water.
2. Lay the wet paper on a desk top or drawing board and smooth out all wrinkles.
3. Blot up any pools of water with the blotting material.
4. Paint directly on this damp paper. Make sure to use more pigment than water, for colors tend to lose their brilliance when dry. Paint the light colors first, and add second and third colors before paper dries, so colors will mingle and blend into spontaneous and soft shapes. After paint is applied, avoid reworking.
5. Leave some areas unpainted to add sparkle.
6. Details, if necessary, can be painted in when the painting is dry.

Note: Damp paper watercolors must be painted hurriedly to be lively. Don't expect complete success on the first try, for only experience will tell just how wet the paper must be and how much paint to use. Clean the brush and the water in the container often.

supplies

1. Transparent watercolors
2. Brush
3. Drawing paper.
4. Water container
5. Blotting material (rag, sponge, paper towels, etc.)

supplies

1. Wax paper or wax stencil paper
2. Paper
3. Pencil
4. Transparent watercolors
5. Brush
6. Water container

watercolor wax resist

procedure

1. Place wax paper over the drawing paper.
2. Draw heavily on the wax paper with pencil or the wooden end of a brush. The pressure will transfer the wax to the drawing paper.
3. Remove the wax paper and paint over the drawing with transparent watercolor. The lines drawn with the pencil will remain white.

Note: Drawing with paraffin or a wax candle will achieve the same result as the wax paper.

paper and cardboard

cardboard relief

supplies

1. Soft cardboard (tablet backing, shirt boards, etc.)
2. Glue
3. Scissors
4. Paint
5. Brush

procedure

1. Cut a cardboard base on which to build a design.
2. Cut a second piece of cardboard into shapes of different sizes and glue to the cardboard base.
3. Cut a third piece of cardboard into shapes smaller in size than the previous pieces and glue in place.
4. Continue to cut and glue smaller pieces until a design of different levels results.
5. Cut and add details, if necessary.

colored tissue paper

procedure

Method A

1. Fold and cut (or sketch, then cut) simple, bold shapes from colored tissue.
2. Arrange these shapes on a white mounting board, overlapping to achieve the most pleasing design and color effects.
3. Cover the tissue paper shapes with rubber cement and gently adhere them to the mounting board.

Note: Boxes, jars, bottles, and trays may be sprayed with white enamel and then decorated in the above manner. Articles to be decorated must be clean and sprayed according to the directions on the can of enamel. Apply tissue shapes that have been coated with rubber cement to the article, spreading smooth so that there are no wrinkles. Remove excess rubber cement with a ball of dried rubber cement, using care, as the tissue tears easily. If desired, additional decorative effects may be added with gold paint and brush to highlight tissue designs. When the paint is dry, spray the entire article with clear enamel to protect designs. Several thin coats, allowed to dry between applications, are necessary. Spray with optimum ventilation.

Method B

1. Cover the board with a thin solution of the glue and water.
2. Cut or tear pieces of colored tissue; press these in place on the glue-covered board while glue is wet.
3. Add additional layers of the paper with glue solution between each layer, until the desired richness of color is achieved.
4. Apply clear spray to protect the design.

Note: Colored tissue paper may be used to decorate a wide variety of items in the home, such as mirrors, wastebaskets, planters, recipe boxes, etc.

supplies

1. Colored tissue in many colors
2. Rubber cement
3. Sharp scissors
4. White mounting board
5. Small brush

supplies

1. Colored tissue in desired colors
2. Mounting board, canvas board, heavy cardboard
3. White glue
4. Clear spray
5. Scissors

1. Tissue paper in many bright colors
2. Fine and medium basket reed
3. Masking tape
4. Rubber cement or white glue
5. Sharp scissors

colored tissue transparent discs

procedure

1. Soak the larger reed in water until it can be bent into circles without breaking. (A fine reed may bend without being soaked.)
2. Cut to make the size circle desired, using the fine reed for the small circles and the medium reed for the larger ones.
3. Overlap the ends of the reed at least one-half inch on the small circles and more on the larger ones, then fasten with small strips of masking tape. Allow the reed to dry thoroughly. (It may be easier to allow the reed to dry partially before fastening with masking tape, as the tape will hold better.)
4. Cut a circle out of tissue paper a little larger than the reed frame.
5. Apply white glue or rubber cement to the reed and press onto the tissue circle.
6. Cut tissue designs in various colors.
7. Cover the design with rubber cement and place on tissue circle. Two, three, or more tissue designs may be placed one on top of another to achieve a really beautiful effect. These may be of the same color or different colors. Only by experimenting can the possibilities be realized.
8. Trim away the tissue extending beyond the frame.

Note: Above all, for the best results, work neatly. Draw the circles with a compass and handle the tissue gently when applying rubber cement. The decorative discs may be used as units in a mobile, to decorate windows, plastic bottles, glass panels, or put on straight reed stems and arranged in a container as a bouquet. They will resemble decorated lollipops!

corrugated cardboard

procedure

Method A

1. Cut out pieces of colored construction paper, corrugated cardboard, or both.
2. Paste these pieces on a piece of corrugated cardboard to form the desired pattern.
3. Accents can be added with ink, tempera paint, or crayon.

supplies

1. Corrugated cardboard
2. Scissors
3. Colored paper
4. Paste or rubber cement
5. Ink, paint, or crayon

Method B

1. Cut through the paper surface of a corrugated cardboard box with a *sharp knife* and peel out areas to expose the corrugations.
2. Color can be added with paints or crayons when the picture is complete.

supplies

1. Corrugated cardboard box
2. Sharp knife
3. Paint, ink, or crayons

supplies

1. Corrugated cardboard
2. Tempera paint
3. Brush
4. Water container

Method C

1. Interesting effects are created by painting directly on the corrugated cardboard. Try painting in the ridges, on top of the ridges, or across the ridges. Further interest may be obtained by using one color inside the ridges and another one on top of the ridges.

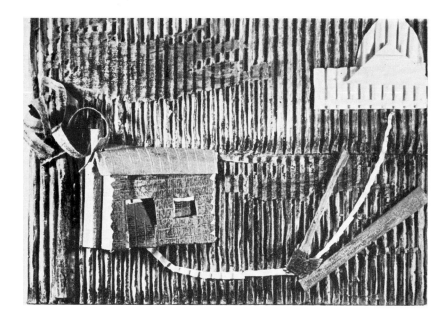

cut paper design

procedure

1. Fold the paper into eighths as in illustration (Ill. 1).
2. Cut numerous small shapes out of the paper until there is more paper cut away than there is remaining (Ill. 2).
3. Carefully unfold the paper so as not to tear it when opening.
4. The design can be mounted on a contrasting colored paper. Numerous designs can be created through an inventive approach using variously colored, shaped pieces under the cut design (Ill. 3).

supplies

1. Thin paper
2. Scissors
3. Rubber cement

1

2

3

cut paper rubbings

supplies

1. Scissors
2. Crayons
3. Drawing paper
4. Construction paper
5. Rubber cement

procedure

1. Cut related shapes from pieces of construction paper (Ill. 1).
2. Arrange the shapes on another piece of paper (if desired, the pieces may overlap) (Ill. 2).
3. Fix the pieces in place with rubber cement.
4. Place another piece of paper over the affixed shapes (Ill. 3).
5. Rub crayons over the paper, using overlapping strokes. The images of the cut shapes will appear (Ill. 4).

Note: Textures may be rubbed onto a piece of paper from any rough surface by laying the paper over the object and rubbing the paper with pencil, crayon, or other drawing instrument.

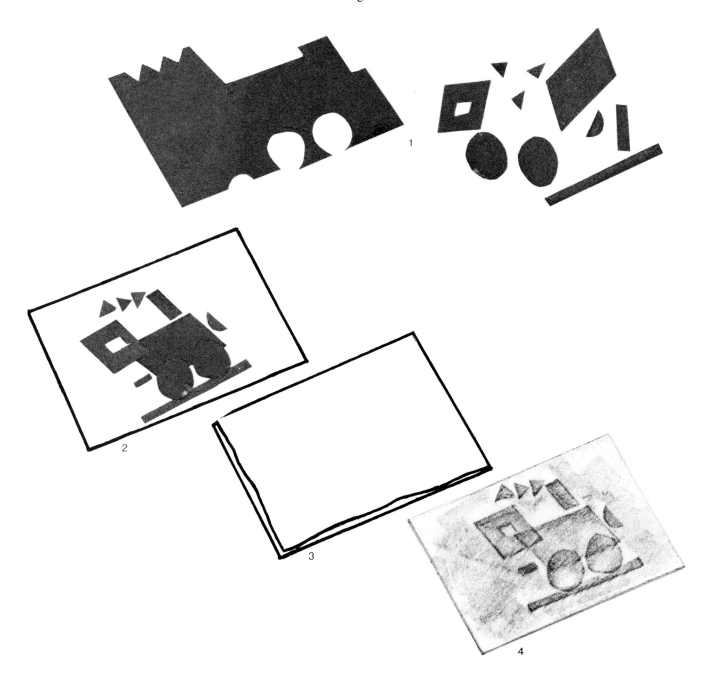

distance silhouette

procedure

1. Make an outline drawing on paper with pencil.
2. Cut out the shapes to appear in the background and rubber cement them to a sheet of white paper (Ill. 1).
3. Place a piece of the translucent paper over the cutout shapes, and hold in place by folding over and gluing to the back (Ill. 2).
4. Cut out shapes and rubber cement these for the middle ground of the original drawing on the above translucent paper (Ill. 3).
5. Cover this with another translucent paper and hold it in place by folding over and gluing to the back (Ill. 4).
6. Complete the picture by rubber cementing objects on the top of the translucent paper (Ill. 5).

Note: As long as the first silhouette is visible through the translucent paper, the procedure can be continued. Translucent paper, which is too heavy, reduces the number of silhouettes. Designs cut from colored cellophane and placed between translucent paper make interesting transparent window decorations.

supplies

1. Colored paper
2. Scissors
3. Translucent paper (tracing paper, onion skin paper, tissue paper, etc.)
4. Rubber cement

1

2

3

4

5

geometric design

procedure

1. Cut geometric shapes that are varied in size and color. Cutting some of these shapes into halves or quarters not only offers more variety of shapes but also correlates well with the teaching of fractions.
2. Group a number of geometric shapes together until they form a picture.
3. When satisfied with the arrangement, paste the shapes in place on background paper.

supplies

1. Colored paper
2. Scissors
3. Paste

1. Colored magazine letters to be used as texture
2. Scissors
3. Paste
4. Sheet of white or colored paper for background

letter collé

Collé is a technique invented by the early cubists in which scraps of papers are pasted to the canvas to provide decorative and tactile embellishments. This is in contrast to another French word "collage," which pertains to the use of various scrap materials.

procedure

1. Select a number of magazine letters of various sizes and colors.
2. Cut out selected letters.
3. Combine two or more letters to create figures, scenes, or a design.
4. Arrange this group of letters on a piece of background paper.
5. Paste the letters in place when satisfied.

magazine collé

Collé is a technique invented by the early cubists in which scraps of paper are pasted to the canvas to provide decorative and tactile embellishments.

procedure

1. Select a number of magazine pictures containing areas that may be used for textural effects.
2. Cut these areas into shapes that, when combined, will create a scene or design.
3. Arrange these paper shapes on background paper.
4. Paste the paper shapes in place when satisfied.

Note: Do not use the texture to create the subject matter from which it came—instead adapt it to other uses (i.e., an illustration of cornflakes could be cut to represent a plowed field, hay stack, rumpled hair, etc).

supplies

1. Colored magazine pictures, to be used as texture
2. Scissors
3. Paste
4. Sheet of white or colored paper for background

procedure

1. Cut lightly into the surface and around each shape that has been previously drawn on colored mat board.
2. Peel out each area after it has been cut.
3. Contrasting color areas can be added with colored paper, paint, or crayon.

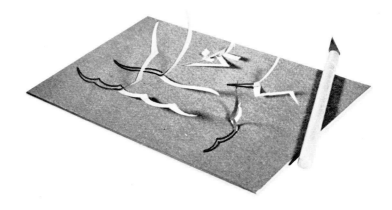